superseries

D1337560

Building the Team

FIFTH EDITION

Published for the
Institute of Leadership & Management

D1337663

ELSEVIER

AMSTERDAM • BOSTON • HEIDELBERG • LONDON • NEW YORK • OXFORD
PARIS • SAN DIEGO • SAN FRANCISCO • SINGAPORE • SYDNEY • TOKYO

Pergamon Flexible Learning is an imprint of Elsevier

Pergamon
Flexible
Learning

Pergamon Flexible Learning is an imprint of Elsevier
Linacre House, Jordan Hill, Oxford OX2 8DP, UK
30 Corporate Drive, Suite 400, Burlington, MA 01803, USA

First edition 1986
Second edition 1991
Third edition 1997
Fourth edition 2003
Fifth edition 2007

Editor: David Pardey

Based on material in previous editions of this work

The views expressed in this work are those of the authors and do
not necessarily reflect those of the Institute of Leadership &
Management or of the publisher

Notice
No responsibility is assumed by the publisher for any injury and/or damage to persons or
property as a matter of products liability, negligence or otherwise, or from any use or operation
of any methods, products, instructions or ideas contained in the material herein

British Library Cataloguing in Publication Data
A catalogue record for this book is available from the British Library

Library of Congress Cataloguing in Publication Data
A catalogue record for this book is available from the Library of Congress

ISBN 978-0-08-046412-1

For information on all Pergamon Flexible Learning publications
visit our website at http://books.elsevier.com

Institute of Leadership & Management
Registered Office
1 Giltspur Street
London
EC1A 9DD
Telephone: 020 7294 2470
www.i-l-m.com
ILM is part of the City & Guilds Group

Typeset by Charon Tec Ltd (A Macmillan Company), Chennai, India
www.charontec.com
Printed and bound in Great Britain

07 08 09 10 11   10 9 8 7 6 5 4 3 2 1

Contents

Contents

Reflect and review   111

Series preface

Whether you are a tutor/trainer or studying management development to further your career, Super Series provides an exciting and flexible resource to help you to achieve your goals. The fifth edition is completely new and up-to-date, and has been structured to perfectly match the Institute of Leadership & Management (ILM)'s new unit-based qualifications for first line managers. It also harmonizes with the 2004 national occupational standards in management and leadership, providing an invaluable resource for S/NVQs at Level 3 in Management.

Super Series is equally valuable for anyone tutoring or studying any management programmes at this level, whether leading to a qualification or not. Individual workbooks also support short programmes, which may be recognized by ILM as Endorsed or Development Awards, or provide the ideal way to undertake CPD activities.

For learners, coping with all the pressures of today's world, Super Series offers you the flexibility to study at your own pace to fit around your professional and other commitments. You don't need a PC or to attend classes at a specific time – choose when and where to study to suit yourself! And you will always have the complete workbook as a quick reference just when you need it.

For tutors/trainers, Super Series provides an invaluable guide to what needs to be covered, and in what depth. It also allows learners who miss occasional sessions to 'catch up' by dipping into the series.

Super Series provides unrivalled support for all those involved in first line management and supervision.

Unit specification

Title:	Building the team		Unit Ref:	M3.11
Level:	3			
Credit value:	1			

Learning outcomes *The learner* will	Assessment criteria *The learner* can *(in an organization with which the learner is familiar)*	
1. Understand how to develop and maintain trust at work	1.1	Explain behaviours which could develop and maintain trust at work
	1.2	Explain why confidentiality is important in building and maintaining trust in the team
2. Know how to build the team	2.1	Give *one* example of a group and *one* example of a team within the workplace. Justify the classification of examples given
	2.2	Briefly describe the stages of an established model of group formation
	2.3	Explain how a manager could benefit from knowing team members' preferred team roles

Workbook introduction

1 ILM Super Series study links

This workbook addresses the issues of *Building the Team*. Should you wish to extend your study to other Super Series workbooks covering related or different subject areas, you will find a comprehensive list at the back of this book.

2 Links to ILM qualifications

This workbook relates to the learning outcomes of Unit M3.11 Building the team from the ILM Level 3 Award, Certificate and Diploma in First Line Management.

3 Links to S/NVQs in management

This workbook relates to the following Units of the Management Standards which are used in S/NVQs in Management, as well as a range of other S/NVQs:

B6. Provide leadership in your area of responsibility
D6. Allocate and monitor the progress and quality of work in your area of responsibility

4 Workbook objectives

> 'Working as a team means flexibility of treatment and people always give their best when they believe they are valued as individuals. Nobody wants to be the same as anyone else. We all start with different basic ideas and it is weaving these ideas together into a dynamic whole which makes for the successful team.'
>
> John Harvey-Jones (1995), *All Together Now*, Mandarin

Every team is a collection of unique human beings each with a contribution to make. Getting the most from the team means combining the talents of all the members in a way that is best fitted to achieving the common task. This must be done while bearing in mind individual needs and ambitions.

In this workbook we will look at the characteristics of work teams, their problems, strengths and weaknesses, and what goes on in them. Most importantly, we will try to find ways of improving the efficiency and effectiveness of teams.

Session A begins by defining the words 'team' and 'work team'. Then we list and compare the different kinds of work teams. The session continues with the subjects of needs and responsibilities: what do people get out of working in a team, what do they need to make it work, and what are they answerable for?

The next session is concerned with behaviour. It covers the stages of team development, the roles people take on in teams, and the norms they are expected to conform to. Next, the question is asked: 'Why do teams fail?'

The third session is about leading and developing teams. We look at maintaining trust and respect, cohesiveness, conflict, and psychometric testing.

4.1 Objectives

When you have completed this workbook you will be better able to:

- assess the needs, responsibilities and motivations of your work team;
- deal with the problems that arise from the way in which people in work teams relate to each other;
- recognize and influence the stages of team development;
- improve the performance of your work team.
- describe the types of structure which form the basis of relationships in organizations;
- develop qualities and skills that will promote positive team relationships.

5 Activity planner

You may want to look at the following Activities now, so that you can start collecting material as soon as possible:

Activity 18 on page 45 in which you are asked to explain how you go about consulting with team members, keeping them informed, honouring your commitments and holding the team's respect.

Activity 19 on page 47 asks you about your approaches to conflict.

Activity 40 on page 88 asks you to review your personal qualities in building a positive environment for your team.

All these Activities may provide the basis of evidence for your S/NVQ portfolio. All Portfolio activities and the Work-based assignment are signposted with this icon.

The icon states the elements to which the Portfolio activities and Work-based assignment relate.

The Work-based assignment (on page 109) suggests that you provide a description and an analysis of a team you lead or belong to. You may want to prepare for it in advance.

Session A
What teams are

1 Introduction

> ' "The joy of working harmoniously with small groups of people who are dedicated to something bigger than themselves, and are completely loyal to each other, counts in my experience as one of the most rewarding things in life," a senior manager told me. Most of us would agree with him.'
>
> John Adair (1987), *Effective Teambuilding*, Pan

There's no doubt that a team that is working well can accomplish great things, and belonging to such a team is a satisfying experience. As we will discover, success is largely determined by the way people behave and how well their needs are met.

We'll look at the needs of teams in this session, but before we do we have to decide what we mean by a team. We all have our favourite teams, and perhaps our favourite groups. Yet how many of us could define the words 'team' and 'group'?

There are many kinds of teams: small teams, and large teams; temporary teams, and long-standing teams; teams that are drilled to work with precision, and teams that falter and fumble; dynamic teams and lazy teams.

What makes a team special? What is the secret of success? These are not easy questions, but if we want to know how to run and participate in teams successfully, we must search for answers.

2 What is a team?

A team is a group of people; so if we want to define what a team is, we could start by saying what a group is.

The first definition of the word 'group' listed in the *Concise Oxford Dictionary* is: 'a number of persons or things located close together, or considered or classed together'. But does this define a team?

Activity 1

4 mins

Tick which of the following groups you would classify as a team.

- The runners in a marathon race. ❑
- A group of volunteers staffing a charity shop. ❑
- The members of two families attending a wedding. ❑
- Eight nurses working on a hospital children's ward, not always on the same shift. ❑
- All the stewards and stewardesses of an airline. ❑
- A group of children sharing a ride on a fairground roundabout. ❑

Now try to write down your own definition of what a team is.

_____

_____

_____

Not all these groups are teams. Runners in a race, or people who happen to be attending the same wedding or sharing the same ride are not teams; the other groups listed in the activity all are.

What's the difference, then, between a group and a team?

One difference between these two sets of examples is that the teams mentioned stay together longer than the other groups. But you may know of – or have worked on – short-term projects, in which a team was formed and disbanded within a few weeks or days. So degree of permanence does not offer a clear distinction between teams and groups.

You may have looked up the definition of 'team' in the dictionary. The *Concise Oxford Dictionary* tells us a team is:

- a set of players forming one side in a game (a cricket team);
- two or more persons working together;
- (a) a set of draught animals; (b) one animal or more in harness with a vehicle.'

As we are not currently concerned about cricket players or draught animals, the second definition is the most relevant. Certainly all of our teams are working together. But we should delve a little deeper than this simple definition if we want to be absolutely clear about what a team is and does.

> Thought: what are the common objectives of your team?

'Team' seems easily to trigger other words like 'team spirit' and 'teamwork'; this may give us a clue. Certainly you could say that the members of a team have **common objectives**. The nurses on the children's ward have an objective of caring for a group of sick children; one of the main objectives of the charity volunteers is to raise funds; the stewards and stewardesses all aim to take care of the airline's passengers. However, you might also point out that the marathon runners share the objectives of finishing the race and trying to win, and that the wedding group aim to wish the bride and bridegroom well.

Another valid point is that the members of a team **depend on one another**; most non-team groups are not interdependent. Also, we can say that team members are **selected**, and that they are **willing to work together**. Further, to be a team, the members have to **think of themselves as a team.**

It's possible to bring to mind groups that have some of these characteristics, but only teams have all of them. To summarize, the members of a team:

- have common objectives;
- are dependent on one another in some way;
- are willing to work together;
- go through a selection process;
- think of themselves as a team.

Incidentally this shows up the limitations of a definition that says: 'a team is two or more persons working together'. You might collect together a group of people to work together who:

- are not agreed about objectives; or
- do not depend on one another; or
- are unwilling to work together; or
- are not selected, but just happen to be in the same place at the same time; or
- do not think of themselves as a team.

2.1 Work teams

In this workbook we are concerned with work teams. We can define a work team simply as 'a team in a work situation'. The special characteristics of work teams are that they are (usually) trained, and carry out defined tasks. Thus:

a work team is a group with common objectives, who are willing to work together, are picked and trained to carry out defined tasks, and whose members are dependent on one another's efforts.

One more point is worth mentioning here, before we leave this activity. Did you notice that two of the groups we've classed as teams – the nurses, and the airline stewards and stewardesses – do not necessarily work together at the same time? This is an important fact: you don't have to be close to one another to be dependent on one another. It's quite possible for some members of a team not to even know each other.

Obviously, work teams aren't all the same: there is a great diversity of work teams operating among tens of thousands of organizations.

EXTENSION 1
Wisdom of Teams demonstrates why teamworking is so important for the 21st century. See page 118.

3 Many kinds of work team

There's no such thing as a 'typical' work team, as the following examples show.

EXTENSION 1
The *Gower Handbook of Teamworking* gives a detailed account of the techniques of teamworking.

Carrie works in the canteen of a public school. Her job is to supervise a small team of cooks and kitchen staff in the preparation and serving of school meals. Carrie is firmly in charge, and nothing happens that she doesn't know about. Although several of her team members have been with her for some time, Carrie is in the habit of keeping her eye on all activities very closely. The rest of the staff members are quite used to this, and they always make sure they keep Carrie informed of progress.

In the Maybury Residential Home, David considers himself fortunate in having a team of staff, most of whom are both experienced and extremely capable. He sees himself as 'less of a manager, and more of a facilitator': he spends his time making it possible for the rest of the team to take care of the residents and to make the home run smoothly. The staff work shifts, and if there is any kind of crisis, the most experienced person present takes charge, calling up help as and when it is needed.

On the Doltex project team, there are: Steve and Terri, both software engineers; Kate and Mitch, whose job is to design the hardware; Max, the Marketing representative; Didar, who keeps account of expenditure; Ben, representing Production; Denis, who is called on from time to time to advise on parts sourcing; and Jerry, the Development Manager. Expert assistance from others in the organization may be called upon from time to time. Christine takes the meeting minutes and distributes project papers. Meetings, which are held at irregular intervals, don't always require the whole team to be present. Jerry has the responsibility of seeing that the project is kept on schedule, and of reporting progress to a more senior group. However, he does not attempt to interfere in the work of the others; he sees his main tasks as ensuring that objectives are agreed and clearly stated, and that there is a mechanism for solving problems.

Madge Killet's sales team have to cover the whole of northern England and Scotland. They work on their own for most of the time, and only meet up once every couple of months, when Madge holds a team meeting. Then they review progress, swap leads, and (afterwards) enjoy each other's company socially.

We can have:

- teams working under close supervision;
- teams that largely control their own activities;
- multidisciplinary or multiskilled teams;
- project teams;
- teams that are widely dispersed;
- teams that work very closely together, perhaps in confined spaces or in difficult conditions;
- teams formed for a brief period;
- permanent teams;
- teams that must accomplish one special task;
- teams that perform a thousand tasks a day;
- teams with only two or three members;
- teams with hundreds of members.

No two teams are the same.

If you put your mind to it, no doubt you could think of teams that have characteristics other than those above.

One kind of team that has become very popular is the self-managed work team.

3.1 Self-managed work teams

'Self-Managing Work Teams offer a radical alternative – one which allows individuals to grow beyond their wildest expectations, and at the same time allows unprecedented levels of output and quality improvement.

This is more than just a restructuring, more than simple quality improvement, more than creating a learning organization – it is a completely different way of life.'

Graham Wilson (1995), *Self Managed Team Working*

The traditional role of the manager is changing. In the previous editions of this Super Series workbook, the focus was on the problems of the team leader in controlling and directing the work of the team. Now there is some fairly fundamental restructuring going on in many organizations. Supervisors and managers used to ask the question: 'How can I run and organize my team to best effect?' Now they are just as likely to ask: 'How can I give my team the support and resources they need, so that they can run and organize themselves?'

The idea of self-managed teams is rather scary to those who haven't tried it.

Activity 2 · 3 mins

Jot down **two** or **three** fears that management may have if teams are allowed to manage themselves.

_____

_____

_____

Fears that come to mind are that teams will:

- run out of control or take too much responsibility;
- squabble among themselves and achieve nothing;
- make managers redundant;
- be leaderless and therefore wander off in all directions;
- make no decisions, or the wrong decisions, because they aren't used to decision making.

Let's look at each of these in turn.

When self-managed teams (SMTs) are first set up, they tend to take too little responsibility upon themselves, rather than too much. They need time and encouragement to adjust to their new role. On the other hand, managers are often reluctant to hand over responsibility, and this in itself will prevent SMTs from being fully effective. The hardest part for the manager is to stand back and watch while the team learns from its mistakes.

Self-managed teams must be given the responsibility and authority to achieve their objectives, without interference from management.

When people are given power, responsibility, and clear objectives, they tend to take responsible attitudes. Squabbling is more likely to take place when team members have no defined roles.

Managers do not become redundant by allowing employees to manage their own work. Instead, their role changes to that of:

- facilitating team decisions by pointing it towards the right information;
- ensuring the necessary resources are available;
- supporting the team when it needs help;
- building trust and inspiring teamwork, by encouraging the team to concentrate on the task, rather than on problems or personalities;
- focusing on longer-term planning and the big picture;
- spending more time thinking about the customer and the competition;
- feeding information;
- breaking down the barriers to change.

Just because teams manage themselves, it does not mean to say that they will be leaderless. The majority of SMTs retain or appoint a single permanent leader. Others are led more loosely, such as on a project-by-project basis.

SMTs do not always make the right decisions, but neither do managers. Unless and until teams are empowered to make their own decisions, and allowed to make mistakes, they will not grow and develop. However, it is true that team members, facing all this responsibility and decision making, may be somewhat 'traumatized'. They are just as likely to be nervous of the process as management is.

Self-managed teams need both support and training.

Of course, managers need training, too, so that they can learn how to handle the new relationship.

Now we turn to the factors that affect work teams, and that make one team different from another.

4 Comparing work teams

What makes each work team special? What factors affect the way that a team operates? What is it like working in a particular team?

Activity 3

4 mins

One factor that helps to determine the way in which one team is different from another is the type of work being done. For example, working in an emergency heart surgery team in a hospital would be quite unlike, say, being a member of a team of gardeners working for the local council. We could contrast them by saying that in one there is a high degree of urgency and the team has to work closely together indoors. In the other there is usually little urgency, perhaps little necessity to work together and the job is done outdoors.

There are other factors besides the type of work that affect the way a team operates and behaves. Jot down **three** other factors, in the space below.

_____

_____

_____

_____

There are a number of points you may have considered.

■ **The type of work** may vary in urgency and location, as already mentioned. Other possible differences include those of 'clean' and 'dirty' jobs; physically demanding work compared with sedentary occupations; and 'thinking' and 'non-thinking' jobs.

A team of labourers may not be required to think for themselves, but they could expect to get dirty and to be physically tired at the end of a shift.	A group of managers attending a 'brainstorming' session would stay clean, and they would probably be sitting down all day. Their idea of hard work may consist of coming up with good new ideas for launching a product.

- **The size of the team** is important: being a member of a team of three or four is likely to be quite a different kind of experience from working in a group of twenty or thirty, for instance.

The members of a very small close-knit team have to get on well together and would probably need the minimum amount of supervision.	In a large team the problems of organization increase, communication and interaction between members become more difficult and the team may be divided (intentionally or otherwise) into subgroups.

- **The type of organization** will certainly affect the way a team behaves and operates. Take two teams of clerical workers for instance, one employed by a government department and the other working for a small private company. Their work might have many things in common and the two teams may be similar in size, but they will probably have many differences in objectives, approach to the task, attitude towards people outside the organization and so on.

- **The team's background and history** will help to influence its behaviour.

In a well-established group, especially one with a record of success behind it, members will be confident with each other and of their place within the organization. Sharing experiences helps people to develop a sense of unity.	The members of a newly formed group, or of one with a history of indifferent achievement, may be unsure about their relationships with one another, and even unclear about the goals and purpose of the team.

- **The technology** involved in the work will obviously make a great deal of difference. You could contrast the work of machinists in a highly automated furniture factory, with that of a team of skilled cabinet-makers creating hand-made tables.

In an automated factory, the main focus is on volume of output and consistency of product. The machine operator plays only a small part in the whole process of design and production. When working with a large machine, also there will be a feeling of remoteness: the operator may not even see the final product.	For the craftsperson, the quality of the single product counts above that of quantity. There is much more scope for individual pride and work satisfaction. Time is also far less important. The craftworker is much closer to the work, touching, feeling and inspecting it closely at every stage of development.

Advanced technology often brings great benefits. A designer of golf courses may find that computer-aided design makes his job easier without making the activity less creative.

■ One other factor that affects the way that a team operates and behaves is **the organizational culture**. (Another closely linked factor is the team culture, but we'll leave discussion of this until Session C.) Organizational culture varies, depending on the history and management style of the organization, the kind of work done and so on. It is difficult to define in a few words precisely what we mean by organizational culture, but the following quotation from Professor Charles Handy sums it up very well.

> 'Culture by definition is elusive, intangible, implicit and taken-for-granted.' – T Deal and AA Kennedy

'In organizations, there are deep-set beliefs about the way work should be organized, the way authority should be exercised, people rewarded, people controlled … What combination of obedience and initiative is looked for in subordinates? Do work hours matter, or dress, or personal eccentricities? … Do committees control, or individuals? Are there rules and procedures or only results? These are all parts of the culture of an organization.'

Charles Handy (1999), *Understanding Organizations*, 4th edition, Penguin (pp 181–182)

Activity 4 · 4 mins

Some indicators of organizational culture are listed below. Think about each one, and give your own organization a mark out of 10.

■ The extent to which information is shared across the organization, and between levels of hierarchy. (All non-confidential information is shared = 10; none is shared = 0.)

■ How much emphasis is placed on quality of product or service, and on caring for the customer. (Quality and the customer always come first in priority = 10; they always come last = 0.)

■ The extent to which encouragement is given for ideas to be generated from below, rather than from above. (Every encouragement = 10; no encouragement = 0.)

■ The level of motivation and responsibility of employees, and how well empowered they are to control their own work. (Totally motivated and empowered = 10; zero motivation or empowerment = 0.)

■ The willingness of people to work together to solve problems. (Everyone is willing and ready to put in their efforts = 10; nobody cares = 0.)

Total

The response to these questions can be found on page 123.

To summarize this section on the factors affecting work teams, we've talked about the:

■ type of work;
■ size of the team;
■ type of organization;
■ team's background and history;
■ technology;
■ organizational culture.

We'll have more to discuss about these and related points later in the workbook. Let's turn our attention for the time being to the needs of team members.

5 The needs of people in teams

Improvements in performance will be the main reason for an organization supporting the development of teams, but there are personal benefits for the individuals concerned too.

Activity 5

3 mins

What do you think people gain from being a member of a team? Write down **two** or **three** benefits of belonging to a team.

_____

_____

_____

_____

Most people enjoy belonging to a group or a team. They gain companionship and a feeling of being part of something. Individuals in a close-knit team learn from each other and support each other. Teams can achieve what a collection of individuals can't.

When the team is well-run, hard-working and forward-looking, the rewards for the individual can be even greater: belonging to a 'winning' team is nearly always an enriching experience.

In summary, the benefits to an individual of being in a team are:

- **companionship**;
- **a sense of purpose**;
- **support**;
- **a sense of belonging**;
- **assistance with problems**.

These benefits have positive effects on morale and motivation. In particular:

companionship and a sense of belonging are very important motivating factors.

Activity 6 · 3 mins

What does the team need? Think now about the needs of a team as a whole, as distinct from the needs of individuals in the team. Jot down **two** or **three** ideas you may have.

_____

_____

_____

_____

Are these the needs of your team?

There are some needs that I would say apply to teams rather than team members. You may agree with me that a team needs the following.

■ **Clear objectives and terms of reference**

A team has to be clear about what it is supposed to achieve, the scope of its work, and where it fits in with other teams.

■ **Support from management, and adequate resources**

If a team is left to run in a vacuum it cannot be expected to produce the required results.

■ **A base – a 'territory' of its own**

This is particularly important for permanent teams, especially where rival teams exist. Most groups of people working or playing together tend to gravitate towards some meeting point. Sports teams usually have a home ground where they will generally expect to be more successful than when 'playing away'. Children who form themselves into groups or 'gangs' will set up private territories with well-defined boundaries, and we can often observe this kind of behaviour in adults. Even dispersed teams, where members do not work in the same place together, may have a location where everyone meets from time to time.

A geographical home base is not always essential. Some teams 'meet' by logging on to a computer network, where they perhaps exchange views and ideas in an informal way – they have a 'virtual' home base. Others have no option but to keep in touch by telephone and post.

■ **A means of identification**

A team needs a name by which they can be recognized as a separate entity. The significance of a name for a team shouldn't be underestimated. Very often it is the only means of providing continuity. For example, some people support the same sports team all their lives, yet the players are changed frequently, as is the management. The team may even move to a different home ground. The only thing that doesn't change is the name.

■ **Stability**

A team that is constantly gaining and losing members will lack continuity; morale and team spirit may suffer. In fact it is possible to destroy team spirit overnight by introducing new personnel or 'transferring' old ones. 'Never change a winning team' seems to be good advice. Nevertheless, no team stays together for ever. It's one of the challenges of leadership to maintain a sense of continuity even when people are moving in and out of the team. The biggest upheaval of all can take place when the leader changes. This is the time when the unity of the team is under greatest pressure.

■ **Leadership**

Do teams need leadership? We have already seen that there is a move to self-managed teams, but that teams without appointed leaders usually elect one, so it seems that they do need leadership. Reporting, and interfacing with other teams, is also usually easier when there are leaders. And a leader is likely to provide a focal point or 'pivot' for a team. We'll have more to discuss about leaders and leadership in Session C.

6 The responsibilities of people in teams

A discussion of team leadership should most definitely not imply that other team members can off-load responsibility, so we will look first at the responsibilities common to the whole team.

Activity 7

List **two** or **three** responsibilities that every work team member has.

_____

_____

_____

_____

You may have responded by saying that a team member has a responsibility to:

■ **communicate** with the team leader and the other members of the team;

■ **share** in the work and in supporting other members;

■ **co-operate** with the rest of the team;

■ **contribute** whatever he or she is able to, in achieving the task.

Thinking about the team as a whole, we could say that everyone in a team has responsibilities towards the following.

■ Achieving **the tasks**: accomplishing the shared tasks is more important than anything else, because the assigned tasks are the reason for the team's existence.

■ Taking a part in the activities of **the group**: when we join a team we have to make a contribution towards that team, without necessarily sacrificing our own individual skills. A football player who is highly talented yet refuses to pass the ball is unlikely to be tolerated for long. Similarly, a work team member who does not co-operate or communicate with the rest of the team makes life difficult for everyone and may even bring progress to a halt.

■ Supporting the **individuals** within the group: a team must be mutually supportive. In fact, the more that the members depend upon each other, the greater will be the bonds between them and the more effective the team will be.

Every team has responsibilities towards the task, the group and the individual.

We have emphasized the importance of communication and interaction between team members. But to what extent and in what way? Give your opinion on the following case history.

Activity 8 ·

10 mins

Ron Preston was a 'bit of a loner', as his colleagues used to say. Ron was not a natural talker and tended to 'keep himself to himself'. He was very proficient on the technical side of what he did, but he didn't mix very much socially with the rest of the team.

Ron's team leader was concerned about this and, because the rest of the team were very sociable, felt that Ron didn't really fit in.

Imagine Ron was on your team. Bearing in mind the responsibilities we've listed above, would you take any action about Ron? Would you perhaps insist he communicate more? Would you go so far as to try to get him moved off the team? Or would you accept Ron for what he was?

_____

_____

_____

Once you have jotted down your response, think whether it is valid for any work situation or whether the response should depend on the circumstances of the job.

_____

_____

_____

We have already discussed the problems that may be caused by poor communication. On the face of things, therefore, a poor communicator is the last kind of member a team needs.

However, in some jobs the only necessary communication is to collect work instructions from the team leader and to report back on what has been done. In others, talking is an essential part of the job, so that poor verbal communicators cannot be tolerated. For example, air traffic controllers have to be in constant dialogue with aircraft pilots, but a lorry driver may only be expected to call into base once during a long trip. In any case, it isn't necessarily important for someone whose job involves talking to be talkative or sociable beyond what the job demands.

You may feel that 'loners' don't fit into most teams, because they contribute too little to team spirit. Communicating doesn't only consist of chatting socially, however. When people are working together in a group they communicate in many ways: by eye contact, through 'body language', with smiles and gestures, by acknowledging each other's presence and simply by observing what the rest of the group are up to.

Team members who do not conform to certain patterns of behaviour don't inevitably cause problems, as perhaps you will agree. The questions to be asked are as follows. Is the team member:

> None of us is perfect, but every team member must contribute to the team's efforts.

- doing what is asked of him or her?
- co-operating with the rest of the team?
- making a full contribution?
- damaging team spirit?

Personality isn't always important: participation is.

Self-assessment 1

10 mins

1 Which six of the following characteristics should be listed in a good definition of a work team?

The members of a work team:

a have a single well-defined task;
b are willing to work together;
c have a history of success;
d manage themselves;
e are trained to carry out defined tasks;
f work together for a long period of time;
g are dependent on one another in some way;
h have common objectives;
i think of themselves as a team;
j work in the same building or area;
k go through a selection process;
l are committed to the leader.

2 In the following grid, there are eight words hidden, which are key to the subject of work teams. (All of them were mentioned in this session.) The words may run forward or backwards, up or down, or diagonally in any direction. See if you can find all eight.

O	G	S	L	I	C	K
T	R	Y	H	I	S	I
W	O	R	K	A	E	T
C	U	L	T	U	R	E
Y	P	A	A	E	I	E
A	A	E	E	S	A	B
R	E	D	A	E	L	M

3 Fill in the blanks in the following sentences with words chosen from the list below:

a _____ teams need both _____ and training.

b Every _____ has responsibilities towards the task, the group and the _____.

c _____ and a sense of _____ are very important motivating factors.

d Self-managed teams must be given the _____ and authority to achieve their _____, without _____ from management.

e _____ isn't always important: _____ is.

BELONGING	COMPANIONSHIP	INDIVIDUAL
INTERFERENCE	OBJECTIVES	PARTICIPATION
PERSONALITY	RESPONSIBILITY	SELF-MANAGED
SUPPORT	TEAM	

Answers to these questions can be found on pages 119–20.

7 Summary

- A work team can be defined as:

  - a group with **common objectives**, who are **willing** to work together, are picked and **trained** to carry out **defined tasks**, and whose members are **dependent** on one another's efforts.

- There are many kinds of work teams, working:

  - with or without supervision;
  - in single-skilled or multiskilled groups;
  - over varying periods of time;
  - in one place or dispersed;
  - to accomplish one or many tasks;
  - with varying numbers of members.

- **Self-managed teams** must be given the responsibility and authority to achieve their objectives, without interference from management. They must be **trained** and **supported**.

- Factors that affect the way a work team behaves and operates include:

  - the type of work;
  - the size of the team;
  - the type of organization;
  - the team's background and history;
  - the technology involved;
  - the organizational culture.

- People gain from being in work teams:

  - companionship;
  - a sense of purpose;
  - support;
  - a sense of belonging;
  - assistance with problems.

- **Teams need**:

  - clear objectives and terms of reference;
  - support from management, and adequate resources;
  - (ideally) a base – a 'territory' of their own;
  - a means of identification;
  - stability;
  - leadership.

- People in work teams have a **responsibility to**:

  - communicate with the team leader and the other members of the team;
  - share in the work and in supporting other members;
  - co-operate with the rest of the team;
  - contribute whatever he or she is able to, in achieving the task.

- In addition, every team has responsibilities towards the **task**, the **group** and the **individual**.

Session B
How teams behave

1 Introduction

> 'The crunch question in the long run is not … what a prospective employee knows, or what specialist skills are possessed: what matters most, given a fair field of adequately qualified candidates, is how the chosen person is going to behave.'
>
> Meredith Belbin (1995),
> *Team Roles at Work*, Butterworth-Heinemann

People don't all react in the same way to situations, events, places or to one another. That's why an insight into what makes each person special is essential to the team leader, if the team is to be fully effective.

Understanding and satisfying the needs of individuals is only one half of the equation, however. There are also many obligations that arise from team membership. Each person must contribute to the team's efforts in his or her own unique fashion.

2 The stages of team development

Four main stages of development in a team or group have been identified. They are: **forming**, **storming**, **norming** and **performing**. A fifth possible stage is **mourning.**

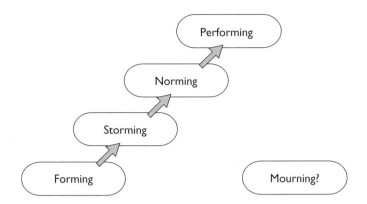

The characteristics of these stages are as follows.

2.1 Forming

At the formation stage, members are:

- finding their feet;
- identifying the task, the boundaries and the rules;
- trying to find ways of approaching the task;
- identifying what information and resources will be needed;
- getting to know one another;
- looking for guidance from the leader;
- learning what kind of behaviour is appropriate.

Some of the worries and concerns at this stage are as follows.

- 'Why am I in this group, and will I fit in?'
- 'What are our aims and objectives?'
- 'Can these aims and objectives really be achieved?'
- 'Am I up to the job?' or perhaps 'Am I capable of more than this?'
- 'How will my performance be assessed?'
- 'How will this group be better than, or different from, the one I've just left?'
- 'How will I get on with the leader and with the other team members?'
- 'Is joining this team good for my career?'

Setting objectives

Fundamental to running a successful work team is knowing what your aims and objectives are, and conveying these aims and objectives to the team.

A work team that is unclear about its reason for existence has little chance of succeeding.

2.2 Storming

During the storming stage, the team are trying to establish relationships with one another. There may be:

- a flaring-up of emotion and conflict;
- a reaction against the demands or value of the task;
- conflict between sub-groups;
- challenges to the position of the leader;
- a reaction against the demands placed on individuals.

The issues here include the question of dominance.

- 'Who is in charge?'
- 'To what extent can I – or do I want to – control the others?'
- 'To what extent will they be able to control me?'

Activity 9   3 mins

How might conflict show itself during the storming stage, do you think? Jot down your ideas, briefly.

_____

_____

_____

The conflict may be open and obvious: disagreement and argument among the members, which in extreme cases may lead to personal hostility and aggression. There may well be a division into two or more 'sides', each representing certain opinions.

The conflict also takes place within the minds of individuals and the symptoms, such as the ones listed below, may not be so obvious:

- Nervousness.
- A reluctance to get on with the job.
- Sullenness.
- Spending excessive amounts of time on trivial tasks.
- Not taking part in group discussions.

These may all be signs of a lack of an individual's ability to get to grips with the real issues.

2.3 Norming

A norm can be defined as a standard of behaviour that is derived from what the members of the group perceive as being acceptable and appropriate.

The norming stage is the period where the members of a group are beginning to work and act like a team. During this 'settling-down' stage, the team is:

■ developing cohesiveness as a group;
■ co-operating and exchanging ideas and opinions about the task;
■ laying down standards and norms;
■ encouraging mutual support.

At this stage, the attention of team members tends to turn to trust, bonding and mutual recognition.

■ 'What is the right way of doing this?'
■ 'Whom can I rely on?'
■ 'Will these relationships develop into real understanding?'
■ 'Will the others recognize my strengths – and overlook my weaknesses?'

This stage is completed when the members have confidence in the team and the contributions they are each to make. This confidence might show itself as:

■ a willingness to listen to the opinions of others;
■ a pride in the team;
■ genuine cohesiveness and a readiness to share;
■ mutual support;
■ a readiness to get on with the job.

The main danger, as group standards are established, is that the norms might not be compatible with the aims and objectives of the organization.

2.4 Performing

This is the stage during which real progress is made, as:

■ solutions begin to emerge;
■ constructive work forges ahead;
■ members take on positive functional roles;
■ group energy is directed towards the completion of the task.

During the performing stage the team and its leader must work just as hard as before at:

- monitoring the output and quality of the work, to ensure it meets targets;
- ensuring performance is maintained;
- seeking new challenges and targets, so that performance can be improved.

A team that is not developing is stagnating.

Good teams are always striving to reach their peak. This can be observed in the very best sports teams. Other sides have a good season and get overconfident: the manager relaxes, the players look for rewards, perhaps the team even starts breaking up. The best teams win consistently, because they are never quite satisfied with their performance.

Winning next time is more important than winning last time.

It won't always be obvious when one stage ends and another begins. Some groups may never fully recover from stage 2, even when progress continues through the last two stages. In other groups, the period of storming may not exist at all.

When you form a new group, or join an existing group as its new leader, you will naturally be anxious to get to the performing stage as quickly as possible. It may not be wise, however, to try to suppress any contentious issues that arise on the way. It is usually best to address the problems, rather than try to pretend they don't exist.

Tackle the problems during team development – or they may reappear.

Activity 10 · 3 mins

Which stages would you assume the following teams have reached, judging from their behaviour? Tick the appropriate box.	Forming	Storming	Norming/ Performing
A team is seen to be continually arguing.			
The members seem to be excessively polite to one another.			
In this team, the members are discussing, freely and constructively, the value of the procedures they are expected to follow.			

Answers to these questions can be found on page 123.

Your assumptions about the statements in this Activity could be wrong, as teams do not always conform to the same patterns of development. For one thing, a team may get stuck in one phase or another.

If your team members go on being polite to one another, for example, and never argue, they may need some extra stimulus in order to move on from the forming to the storming stage.

A level of turbulence is often necessary to bring out the best in people.

On the other hand, if there is a lot of conflict, which you perceive to be largely destructive, it's possible that too much personal animosity exists between some members. If that's the case, the team may never settle down to productive working relationships, unless a strong leader manages to gel the team together.

We will look at the topic of dealing with conflict in Session C.

2.5 Mourning

A final phase in development is team disbandment – what may be called the **mourning** stage.

Activity 11

3 mins

Suppose a team is disbanded, and everyone goes on to join other teams. What factors do you think will affect the members' behaviour and performance in the new teams?

_____

_____

_____

_____

You may agree that there are several possible factors, such as the following.

- How well did the original team perform? If it did well, the members would probably have a high level of confidence for the next venture, whereas if things went badly, that confidence may be missing.
- What happened when the team broke up? It's possible to handle the winding up of a team well or badly. The sudden imposed dispersal of a successful, long-standing team may actually cause the members to feel as though they are in mourning.
- The hopes and expectations of the new teams.

What's the best way to disband a team? Alison Hardingham and Jenny Royal in their book _Pulling Together_ (1994), suggest that teams should:

- **plan for the end as early as possible**, as people like to have clear plans, and time to get used to the idea;
- **provide a formal opportunity for members to say what they have valued about each other as colleagues, and what they will miss –** both on the personal level and the professional;
- **warn the team that they will feel sad**;
- **hold a final dinner or lunch**; a 'ritual' can help relieve feelings;
- **encourage team members to stay in touch** as individuals.

If the team has been successful, you have reason to congratulate one another, and you may want to mark the breaking up of the team with a fair amount of ceremony and celebration.

> 'There is no failure except in no longer trying.' – Elbert Hubbard, *The Note Book*

But what if the team is seen to have failed? You may agree that, if members have honestly done their best to achieve success, there will almost certainly be some good news among the bad. It is worth recording what you have done well, and what you will do differently next time. At the very least the team can learn something from its mistakes.

Now we have reviewed the stages of development of teams, it's time to look at the behaviour of team members, and the roles they take up.

3 The roles people play

The roles that members adopt in the activities of the team will depend on their personalities, their skills and the expectations of colleagues. Some roles will vary according to circumstances and the demands of the task.

It has been said that everyone, in any situation, takes on a role in relation to other people. There are two sets of influences at work.

- The person's own personality, skills and other attributes.
- The effects of the situation itself, and of the other people involved.

Each of us takes on many different and separate roles throughout our lives.

3.1 Role and status

It is important here to distinguish between role and status. To take an example, a man achieves the status of **fatherhood** as the result of the birth of his child. The role he assumes as a **parent** will depend on many things: what kind of person he is, the behaviour the mother expects of him, the behaviour society expects from fathers generally and so on.

In a similar way, to say that a man or a woman is a team leader is a statement of status, but it tells us nothing about the behaviour of that person. Roles at work depend on (among other things) personality, culture, the requirements of the task, and the influence of colleagues. Status indicates what people **are** – their position in life or at work; the roles they take on help to describe what they **do** and how they **behave.**

Job-related roles are the most obvious, and usually the best defined. A team of road repair workers might have a team leader who directs the work, a man who's skilled with the use of a pneumatic drill, an excavator operator and so on.

A team of operators or technicians may be selected simply on the basis of the specialist skill requirements of the team, so that their job-related roles are clear and unambiguous, and are the most important. They may not normally hold meetings, and perhaps do not even need to communicate with each other very much. Nevertheless, they will still need to trust each other and come to a mutual understanding about their work. That being so, the personality, strengths and weaknesses of each individual will tend to make a difference to the way the team does things.

In other work teams the members are required to co-operate and collaborate with one another a great deal, and, if this is the case, they will depend heavily on one another. A few out of many possible examples are:

- a group of teachers and parents working together to organize a school fete;
- a project team planning the development of a new railway service;
- a team laying a pipeline across a desert;
- a marketing team working together to form a new sales strategy.

In such cases, personalities may be as important as skills, and the interaction of the team members will be a critical factor in determining success.

As with all human relationships, complex forces are at work. Nevertheless, we can benefit by learning to recognize roles, in ourselves and others. People in groups tend to take on different roles according to their experience, personality, training, background and so on. This is normal and necessary. A well-balanced work team depends upon members assuming different roles.

3.2 The 'balanced' team

Some teams are obviously more successful than others. But many organizations have found that variations in results between teams cannot always be explained by differences between the levels of expertise of the teams' members. If there are two teams, each with equally impressive sets of talented people, one team may 'gel' together, while the other does not.

The key to success seems to be to select teams that have not only the necessary skills and knowledge, but that are 'well balanced' in having people who can cover all the required roles. To take a simple example, if all a team's members are natural organizers, and everyone wants to take charge, then conflict may be inevitable. Or if everybody is creative without being good at translating ideas into actions, no useful work may get done at all.

EXTENSION 3
Belbin's team roles are explained in more detail in his book *Team Roles at Work*.

Ideally, every team has 'planners', 'doers', 'ideas people' and so on, so that all the required roles are filled. This concept has been developed by a number of management writers. Perhaps the best known expert in this field is Dr Belbin, who identified nine team roles; they are as shown on page 31.

These are **team roles**, as distinct from job titles or job-related roles. One person on a project team, for example, might combine the technical, job-related role of process engineer, and the team role of monitor/evaluator.

In the ideal team, there will be one or more individuals who fit perfectly into each of Belbin's nine team roles. However, in most real-life teams, not every role will be matched neatly against the characteristic style of a team member.

To some extent, matching people with roles involves knowing the personalities in your team; we will look at this issue in Session C.

Simply recognizing that all these team roles are needed can be helpful. If you can identify the roles that are not being filled, you will know what your team lacks. You and other team members may have to make a conscious decision to take on, say, the 'completer', or the 'shaper', so filling whatever roles are vacant.

Belbin's team role	Description and contribution to team	Allowable weaknesses
Co-ordinator	Clarifies the team's objectives and sets the agenda. Mature, confident, but not domineering – a good chairperson. Promotes decision making and delegates well.	Does not usually generate ideas, and is not necessarily brilliant intellectually. May be seen to be manipulative.
Completer	A painstaking individual – very conscientious, and often anxious. Will personally check all details for errors and omissions. Delivers on time.	A worrier, who is reluctant to delegate. May be over-finicky and hypercritical.
Implementer	Is capable of translating ideas into manageable tasks. Well-organized, disciplined, efficient, trustworthy and reliable. Always knows what's going on.	May be rather inflexible, and slow to respond to alternative proposals.
Monitor/evaluator	Another high IQ person (like the Plant below) who is typically introvert and sober. Good at making sound judgements, and at absorbing and unravelling information.	Unexciting – tends to lack drive, and does not inspire others. May be very critical.
Plant or creator	A creative and imaginative person, who also has a high IQ; original and unorthodox. Solves difficult problems.	Tends to ignore details in favour of large issues; may be too preoccupied to communicate effectively. May be poor at handling criticism.
Resource investigator	A sociable, stable extrovert, who is enthusiastic and communicative, but tends to dominate. Explores opportunities and develops contacts. Needs to be under pressure.	Over-optimistic. Enthusiasm for any topic may not last long.
Shaper	Dominant extrovert, who thrives on pressure. A good task leader, and has the drive and courage to overcome obstacles. May be charming, and have a lot of nervous energy.	Inclined to paranoia, and may either upset or stimulate others.
Specialist	The expert on the team. Usually an introvert, whose interest is confined to own sphere of knowledge. A single-minded self-starter.	May restrict contribution to own field. Focuses only on technicalities, rather than people or the overall project.
Teamworker	As the name suggests, a reliable team player: co-operates willingly, and a good listener and diplomat. Avoids friction and confrontation, and calms the waters. A likeable extrovert.	Although very supportive when the team's in difficulties, does not like making decisions. May be manipulated by others.

Activity 12

Look again at the table on page 31, and try to match Belbin's nine team roles to the members of your own team.

Team role	Who fills it?	Who might fill it?
Co-ordinator		
Completer		
Implementer		
Monitor/evaluator		
Plant or creator		
Resource investigator		
Shaper		
Specialist		
Teamworker		

3.3 Role stress

Sometimes, fulfilling roles can result in stress. For instance, a person may be unhappy in the role he or she is forced or expected to adopt. This may be the result of a difference between personal perception of one's abilities, and other people's assessment. People given a job well above or well below their abilities may be distressed about it.

Another source of stress is **role conflict**, whereby two or more roles clash with one another. For example, a team leader may be trying to help and support a team member, while being urged by management to act as a disciplinarian.

Another kind of role problem is **role overload**. This is not the same as work overload, which is simply the result of having too much to do. Role overload means trying to fulfil too many roles, some of which may be in conflict.

Activity 13

Think about your own job. Spend some time trying to list all the roles you play at work. You may want to include some of the following: peacemaker, confessor, instructor, disciplinarian, administrator, salesperson, subordinate, report writer, information collator, technician, spokesperson, slave(?), organizer, cajoler, computer, messenger …

_____

_____

_____

Are any of these roles in conflict? If so, can you do anything about it: reduce the importance of one of the roles, perhaps?

_____

_____

_____

Do you consider that you suffer from role overload? If so, how might you delegate any of your roles?

_____

_____

_____

3.4 More about roles

Here are some further points about roles and role-playing.

■ Roles are important to the individual and to the team. However, the main issue is the fulfilment of the task. All team members may have to take on roles they don't enjoy, from time to time.

- In determining job-related roles, job descriptions are essential. Everyone at work should be able to refer to a document that outlines their functions and responsibilities. In some cases a job description can set out precisely what has to be done. In others the job description can't be specific, because the role may change according to circumstances. All job descriptions should be written so that there is some scope for personal development.

- Remember that roles are not exclusive to certain individuals and that individuals need not be restricted to certain roles.

- Beware of labelling people. Because a person normally fills a certain role, through either choice or compulsion, it doesn't mean to say that he or she is incapable of a different role.

Role stress often is the result of pressure. One kind of pressure that is nearly always present in teams is peer pressure, arising from group norms.

4 Group norms

'To be nobody-but-myself in a world which is doing its best, night and day, to make you everybody else – means to fight the hardest battle which any human being can fight, and never stop fighting.' – e.e. cummings

A **group norm** can be defined as a standard of behaviour that is derived from what the members of the group perceive as being acceptable and appropriate.

A team's collective perception of what is 'correct behaviour', or the 'right response' in a particular situation, may have a great effect upon the individual, for good or ill. None of us lives in a vacuum: we are all affected by **peer pressure**, i.e. influenced by friends, families and colleagues. By and large, most of us try to do what we think is expected of us.

Every work team will have norms of its own and these norms may, or may not, be in the best interests of the organization as a whole. For example, a team may have norms that affect:

- how much work members do;
- how flexible the team is and how willing it is to accept changes;
- how much thought the team will give to finding new ways of doing things.

Activity 14 ·

3 mins

Jot down **three** or **four** other ways in which a work team's group norms might affect what goes on at work.

_____

_____

_____

_____

_____

There are a number of things you may have suggested, including:

- how easily new members are accepted into the team;
- the language used;
- the way work is performed;
- who does what in the team;
- the standard of dress;
- what people do in the lunch hour.

Once norms have become established, there may be a good deal of pressure on members to conform. This pressure may take a variety of forms, ranging from laughter at non-conforming behaviour or exclusion from 'in-jokes' and conversations, to verbal or physical abuse.

Even when there is no apparent sign of a reaction against those who do not conform, the pressure to obey norms may still be very real. The tendency of most people in most situations is to behave as they see others behaving.

We are all under pressure to conform.

One key task for the work team leader is to take note of any unhealthy group norms that may be developing. Some questions to be asked are these.

- Are the norms in the interests of the team and the organization?
- Is unreasonable pressure being applied to individuals to conform against their will?
- Is a strong minority holding the team back for its own interests?
- Are the norms relevant to the common task?

The team leader needs to be aware of group norms and their effects on the team.

However, group norms aren't always a bad thing, by any means.

Activity 15

Think about your own work team and jot down **two** or **three** norms (standards) that are of positive benefit to the individual and to the team and/or the organization.

_____

_____

_____

_____

You may have suggested:

- safety standards that are acceptable to everyone because they save lives;
- good working practices, which have been derived from experience;
- standards of courtesy;
- standards of hygiene;
- standards of honesty.

You can probably think of many more standards, or norms, that are in the best interests of individuals to follow.

5 Why do teams sometimes fail?

When teams work well, they can achieve remarkable feats. Effective teams can:

- increase an organization's productivity;
- put forward and implement original ideas;

- make half-baked ideas work;
- bring out the best in team members;
- unite a group of disparate individuals;
- raise the morale of a whole organization.

But not all teams are as effective as they might be. What gets in the way of teams performing to their full potential?

Activity 16 · 3 mins

What goes wrong in teams? Jot down **two** or **three** reasons that might prevent a team achieving or exceeding its objectives.

_____

_____

_____

_____

_____

You may have suggested any one of the following reasons for the lack of success of a particular team.

As we go through the points, it would be useful to bear in mind our definition of a team. We said that:

EXTENSION 4
Why Teams Don't Work
is a practical handbook
that shows how a team
can work together to
achieve its goals.

a work team is a group with common objectives, who are willing to work together, are picked and trained to carry out defined tasks, and whose members are dependent on one another's efforts.

If any of these factors is missing, or is not given sufficient consideration, the team will not 'fire on all cylinders'.

- Any team is composed of individuals, each with his or her own ambitions, prejudices, ideas and preferences. None of us is the same as anyone else, and a particular group of people won't necessarily become an effective team. This is especially true if:

  - team members feel they are in competition with one another, perhaps to impress the boss or to gain promotion;

- they aren't encouraged to co-operate;
- the performance of individuals is seen to be rewarded, rather than the whole team being judged on the team's results.

If this kind of situation exists, the team members will not be 'willing to work together', but will tend to work on their own behalf, or even **against** the team.

Sometimes a team leader has to try to forge a winning team from an unlikely bunch of candidates. The good news is that it can quite often be achieved.

- A second possible reason for failure is for team members to be badly selected, or for the wrong type of team to be formed. It is very tempting for organizations, when setting up a new group, to pick people who happen to be available at the time, rather than select them to fill defined roles.

- Another mistake is to set up a team with objectives or terms of reference that are inadequately defined. For example, it has been known for organizations to establish project teams with vaguely stated aims such as: 'To find ways to cut costs' or 'To improve the quality of the product'. Such aims are rarely achieved separately from work processes: the best people to control costs and quality are the teams who are doing the work.

- Lack of training and support for a team may be another route to failure. People need to know how to perform well in their assigned team roles, and what is expected of them. Perhaps you've been part of a team where the questions at the forefront of your mind were:

- 'Why am I here – what am I supposed to do?'
- 'How am I expected to contribute?'
- 'Why is everyone arguing and cross with one another?'

As we discussed earlier in this session, a team will typically go through stages of development of:

- forming: getting to know one another;
- storming: going through a period of conflict as rules and relationships are established;
- norming: settling down;
- performing: working to best effect.

Anyone not experienced or educated in this process will find it harder to fit in, and to understand what's going on. If, on top of this, the team:

- members are inadequately trained in their specialist functions;
- is given insufficient resources and support by management;
- is not empowered to make its own decisions;

then disaster is almost ensured.

■ One other possible reason for lack of team success that you may have mentioned is poor communication within the team and/or between teams.

> Some of the teams in the Questex Development Group were not performing as well as the company's senior management thought they should. A firm of consultants was brought in to investigate, and their report highlighted 'communication problems' as a major factor. Among the reasons listed were:
>
> ■ individuals and teams hoarding information and ideas, on the grounds that they 'didn't trust other people not to claim credit for them'
> ■ information not being passed on, because of the false assumption that others were already aware of it
> ■ dominant individuals imposing decisions on the rest of the team, many of whom were not prepared to question them or speak out against them.

■ A final possible cause of team non-performance that is worth noting at this time is unresolved friction and conflict. A certain amount of conflict is useful, inevitable and even necessary, because it is rare for everyone to have the same views. The best ideas and approaches may appear only after a period of disagreement. But personal antagonism or hostility that is not cleared up amicably may get in the way of progress.

In session C, we will look at ways of dealing with conflict in teams, and at some ideas for ensuring success.

Self-assessment 2

1 Norming, mourning, storming, forming, performing. Place these team development stages in the correct order.

2 Match each Belbin team role with the correct description.

Belbin's team role	Description and contribution to team
1 Monitor/evaluator	a A painstaking individual – very conscientious, and often anxious. Will personally check all details for errors and omissions. Delivers on time.
2 Shaper	b A creative and imaginative person, who also has a high IQ; original and unorthodox. Solves difficult problems.
3 Specialist	c A sociable, stable extrovert, who is enthusiastic and communicative, but tends to dominate. Explores opportunities and develops contacts. Needs to be under pressure.
4 Resource investigator	d Another high IQ person (like the Plant) who is typically introvert and sober. Good at making sound judgements, and at absorbing and unravelling information.
5 Co-ordinator	e As the name suggests, a reliable team player: co-operates willingly, and a good listener and diplomat. Avoids friction and confrontation, and calms the waters. A likeable extrovert.
6 Implementer	f Clarifies the team's objectives and sets the agenda. Mature, confident, but not domineering – a good chairperson. Promotes decision making and delegates well.
7 Completer	g Dominant extrovert, who thrives on pressure. A good task leader, and has the drive and courage to overcome obstacles. May be charming, and have a lot of nervous energy.
8 Teamworker	h Is capable of translating ideas into manageable tasks. Well-organized, disciplined, efficient, trustworthy and reliable. Always knows what's going on.
9 Plant or creator	i The expert on the team. Usually an introvert, whose interest is confined to own sphere of knowledge. A single-minded self-starter.

3 Pick out the correct statements from the following.

a In determining job-related roles, job descriptions are essential.
b A group norm can be defined as a standard of behaviour that is derived from what the group leader perceives as being acceptable and appropriate.
c A possible reason for failure of a team is that team members are badly selected.
d Roles are important to the individual and to the team. However, the main issue is the fulfilment of the task.

Answers to these questions can be found on pages 120–1.

6 Summary

- Four main stages of development in a team or group have been identified. They are: **forming**, **storming**, **norming** and **performing**. A fifth possible stage is **mourning**.

- During 'forming' people join the team and find their place. When 'storming', they are trying to establish relationships; conflict may result. 'Norming' is the stage when team members are settling down and developing cohesiveness. As the name suggests, during 'performing' real progress is made. 'Mourning' occurs when the team is disbanded.

- When plans are made to **disband the team**, it is a good idea to:
  - plan for the end as early as possible, as people like to have clear plans, and time to get used to the idea;
  - provide a formal opportunity for members to say what they have valued about each other as colleagues, and what they will miss – both on the personal level and the professional;
  - warn the team that they will feel sad;
  - hold a final dinner or lunch; a 'ritual' can help relieve feelings;
  - encourage team members to stay in touch as individuals.

- Personalities may be as important as skills, and thus **team roles** may be as significant as job-related roles. In the balanced team, every team has 'planners', 'doers', 'ideas people' and so on, in order that all the required roles are filled.

- The **team roles** suggested by Belbin are: monitor/evaluator; shaper; specialist; resource investigator; co-ordinator; implementer; completer; teamworker; plant or creator.

- Role stress may be present in the form of **role conflict** or **role overload**.

- A **group norm** can be defined as a standard of behaviour that is derived from what the members of the group perceive as being acceptable and appropriate.

- A team may **fail** if: team members are not willing to work together; the members are badly selected; objectives or terms of reference are poorly defined; there is a lack of training or support, or poor communication; there is unresolved personal hostility.

Session C
Leading and developing a team

◼ 1 Introduction

Team development never stops. Ask any football team manager. If you are on a losing run, morale drops and you have to work hard to find ways of coping with the task in hand. Even if you are winning all your matches at the moment, it would be foolish to assume that your run of success will go on indefinitely. Unexpected problems are always emerging and you have to be prepared to deal with them. You must watch for any signs of complacency. The best teams, in fact, work harder at team development when they are winning.

Unlike a football manager, you may not be in the happy position of being able to pick the best players for your team. You perhaps have plenty of ideas people, but no 'striker' – someone who can make sure you reach the goal. Or your team members may be reluctant to 'pass the ball' – they may seem to want to keep things to themselves rather than co-operate.

In this session we will look at the ways a team can develop and grow, from the team leader's point of view. Among other aspects, we discuss trust and **support**, ways of dealing with **personality problems**, and **cohesiveness.**

◼ 2 Your role as team leader

You may be called a manager, a supervisor, or a team leader. Whatever your title, it won't necessarily be obvious to an outsider what exactly your role is, or how you interface with the people who report to you.

Until fairly recently, nearly everyone had a boss who directed and controlled their activities. Now many teams, as we have discussed, are self-managed. This changes the team leader's role to one of **facilitating** the team's activities.

However, all team leaders must:

■ maintain the trust and support of team members; and
■ aim to minimize interpersonal conflict.

2.1 Maintaining trust and support

The following extract describes the importance of the role of the supervisor in relation to the more traditional style of work team.

> 'Attitude surveys within Laing have shown time and time again that job satisfaction is totally correlated to the satisfaction that they have with their immediate superior. Their loyalty first and foremost is going to be to their boss and he represents the company. If they know where they stand, know what is expected of them, see that as being fair and reasonable and feel that in difficulty they will have his support and commitment, then they will give commitment to him and in turn to the team and the company.'
>
> John Armitt, Deputy Managing Director of
> John Laing International Limited,
> quoted in John Adair (1987), *Effective Teambuilding*, Pan

Activity 17

List **two** or **three** responsibilities of a work team's leader, bearing in mind the words in the quotation above.

_____

_____

_____

_____

You may agree that the leader has a responsibility to:

- **demonstrate a commitment** to the team;
- **make clear the roles of the team members**, so that everyone knows what is expected of them;
- **set out the overall and specific aims and objectives**, so that everyone knows what has to be done and why it has to be done;
- **agree objectives** wherever possible, to ensure that what is being asked is fair and reasonable;
- **support the team when things are going against it** and to support the individual (including, if necessary, protecting individuals from the group).

An important aspect of this is maintaining the team's trust and support.

Activity 18

**S/NVQ
B6**

This Activity may provide the basis of appropriate evidence for your S/NVQ portfolio. If you are intending to take this course of action, it might be better to write your answers on separate sheets of paper.

If you are a team leader, explain how you maintain the trust and support of your team members, by responding to the following questions or comments.

a How do you go about consulting with members about proposed activities?

_____

_____

_____

_____

b How do you ensure that those consultations are conducted in an open and frank manner, so that everybody has a chance to express an opinion?

_____

_____

_____

_____

c How do you keep them informed about organizational values, policies and strategies, progress, emerging threats and opportunities?

_____

_____

_____

_____

d Give an example of a commitment or promise that you recently made to team members.

_____

_____

_____

_____

e Explain to what extent you were, or expect to be, able to honour that commitment.

_____

_____

_____

_____

f To what extent would you say that you treat team members with proper respect, and keep their confidences? (One way to tell is to ask yourself whether they treat you with the respect you would like.)

_____

_____

_____

_____

2.2 Dealing with conflict

As mentioned earlier, a certain amount of conflict can be useful and may be unavoidable. We said that:

a level of turbulence is often necessary to bring out the best in people.

The question is: how much conflict is too much? When does conflict become unhealthy, counter-productive or destructive? This may seem difficult to answer, but the signs are always there if you watch out for them.

'Positive' conflict	'Negative' conflict
Conflict is healthy if it is good-natured bantering, or reasoned argument.	It is unhealthy if a great deal of heat is being raised, resulting in people being seriously upset, angry, or even physically hurt.
Conflict is productive if it results, sooner or later, in issues being resolved.	It is counter-productive if it means that people are at loggerheads, and neither side is prepared to give way.
Conflict can be constructive if it allows people to release their feelings and express what they really feel.	It will usually be destructive if it causes some people to clam up and hide their feelings.

There is no doubt that when serious or aggressive interpersonal conflict arises – between individuals, or between opposing sides – it should be stopped as soon as possible.

As the team leader you will need to do the following.

- **Inform team members of the standards of work and behaviour** that are expected of them. There are many ways to do this, and the method you use may vary according to the individual concerned. One of the best ways is by example: your behaviour, your work standards and the kind of language you use, must be at least at the level you expect others to reach.
- **Make sure that team members have an opportunity to discuss problems** that arise, in confidence if necessary.
- **Take prompt action** to deal with serious conflict.
- **Keep your manager informed**, particularly when serious conflict arises. Should conflict result in disciplinary action having to be taken, you must of course follow your organization's policies, and keep within the law. Proper records must also be made.

Activity 19

15 mins

S/NVQ B6

This Activity may provide the basis of appropriate evidence for your S/NVQ portfolio. If you are intending to take this course of action, it might be better to write your answers on separate sheets of paper.

If you have encountered serious interpersonal conflict in a team you were leading, explain the circumstances and what exactly was going on.

_____

_____

_____

_____

How did you deal with this conflict?

_____

_____

_____

_____

From your past experience, explain how you intend to deal with a similar incident in the future.

_____

_____

_____

_____

What recommendations would you make within your organization to improve procedures and reduce the potential for negative interpersonal conflict?

_____

_____

_____

_____

3 Building your team

Most of the time team leaders are not given the opportunity to set up a team from scratch, with a completely free hand. Usually they have to inherit existing teams, and are faced with the daunting task of getting to know a whole group of people while maintaining output and quality. Alternatively, they may be appointed by the team itself.

I expect you agree with me that it is very useful if the team leader can have a say in the selection of the team, or of new members for an existing team. This follows from the fact that the team leader is the one with the ultimate responsibility for the team's performance. Sadly, some organizations take the view that appointment of staff is a senior management function entirely.

Whoever picks the team, it has to be done with care and attention. In an ideal world, the team picked will consist of individuals who have capabilities entirely suited to their role, and whose personalities are totally compatible. In the last session, we looked at Belbin's nine roles, which illustrated the range of roles likely to be needed in a typical team.

In the real world, this happy state of affairs is rarely achieved. Inevitably, in the typical work team:

- personality clashes arise;
- rivalry and perhaps jealousy exist between members;
- people tend not to tackle jobs, or fit into the roles, that do not appeal to them.

There may or may not be any outward signs of conflict: the team members may simply not be working together very well, and productivity may be low.

Activity 20

4 mins

Suggest **two** or **three** useful ways in which the team leader might try to help the team get on better together.

_____

_____

_____

_____

Some useful tips you may have listed are to:

- **emphasize the value and importance of the task**;
- **keep everyone busy**: a busy team is often a happy team;
- **praise loudly, criticize quietly**;
- **encourage friendly rivalry** at the expense of hostility;
- **acknowledge the value of the skills and experience of individuals** and put them to good use in helping others learn;
- **watch out for the emergence of sub-groups**: break them up if necessary by switching assignments.

So far as covering all aspects of the task is concerned – all the roles – you may have suggested using Belbin's team roles as a guide. One difficulty with this approach is that it may be difficult to assess what someone's personality and preferences are, especially if you don't know them well.

One way to assess personality is through **psychometrics.**

Psychometric tests are used to measure various aspects of human personality. The use of these tests is regulated by The British Psychological Society. Psychometrics should be used only to inform team members about likely team strengths and weaknesses, and about the way they can be expected to interact with one another. They should **not** be used to make decisions about people.

3.1 Getting to know your team

If psychometrics is not available to you, you can learn a great deal just by getting to know your fellow team members.

Activity 21

How important do you think it is for a team leader to get to know all team members well, in order to gain a better understanding not only of their abilities, but something of each person's individual temperament, beliefs, motivation and so on?

Very important   Fairly important   Useful but not necessary

     ❐   ❐   ❐

How would you go about this?

_____

_____

_____

I hope you agree with me that it is very important. To build a successful team a team leader must try to get the best from every individual in it. The more the full potential of each team member is realized, the greater will be the benefit to the team. The first step in this process must be for the team leader to begin to understand the individual's strengths and weaknesses, attitudes, ambitions: in short, what makes that person 'tick'.

This doesn't mean prying into members' private lives, or asking lots of searching questions. It's more a process of working with them and observing:

- the way they approach their work;
- their interactions with you and with their workmates;
- their reaction to events and circumstances.

It takes time and conscious effort. There is nothing new about the point I am making here: to a large extent it's what every team leader does all the time. When a team leader assigns tasks and roles to people in the work team, it goes without saying that more attention must be paid to new members whose abilities are unproven, than to those who have already shown what they are capable of.

Nevertheless, it's a common mistake to over-estimate our capacity to judge the capabilities of others, as the following case history illustrates.

> Jon Cooke was a management trainee, employed by a hotel chain. He was given experience in a wide range of jobs in the hotel trade. Jon was naturally shy and suffered from a slight stammer, which didn't always help him when dealing with customers. In addition, during his training period, Jon made a couple of errors of judgement, one of which caused a hotel to run out of food during an important function and the other resulting in overbooking of rooms. At the end of two years, Jon's superior summed up Jon as 'lacking senior management potential', and the hotel organization didn't offer him a permanent position.
>
> In spite of this, Jon knew that he really enjoyed the kind of work he'd been doing. After lots of applications, he was successful in getting appointed as an under-manager with another company. In new surroundings and with a fresh start Jon rose to the position of manager, then area senior manager. Within five years, Jon was on the Board and three years later became Managing Director.

We've all heard stories of this kind, in which the full potential of individuals has not been realized until circumstances change. It has been said that most people, most of the time, fail to realize their full potential. It's something worth bearing in mind.

To get the best from people, you may have to work hard at getting to know them well.

So far in this session, we've looked at maintaining trust and support, dealing with conflict, and getting to know the team. Another important aspect of teambuilding is cohesiveness.

4 Cohesiveness

A team is more than just a collection of individuals. **Cohesiveness** is a quality that can be used to describe how unified a team is. The best teams are highly cohesive, so encouraging and maintaining cohesiveness is an important part of the job of team development.

Cohesiveness might be measured by the importance members place on belonging to the group: how much effort they would make to retain membership.

It is linked to **morale**, as both words have implications about group confidence, enthusiasm and loyalty. Morale is another of those words we use quite freely, but which is hard to define precisely. It can be described as 'how the team thinks and feels about the job they are currently doing'.

It is possible for group morale to be low, and cohesiveness still to remain high. This might happen, for example, where a team feels itself unfairly criticized or under threat.

It's more difficult to imagine circumstances whereby cohesiveness is lacking, while group morale remains high. Cohesiveness seems to be an important part of morale.

How can we recognize whether a high level of cohesiveness exists within a team?

One thing that might give you a clue is the frequency with which the words 'us', 'we' and 'our' are used in conversations compared with 'me', 'I' and 'my'. People who think of themselves as part of a team tend to share everything, tasks, responsibilities, equipment, rewards and so on, and so tend to talk as a unified group.

Activity 22

There are several factors that affect cohesiveness. For instance, the members of a group will tend to get a greater feeling of belonging together if they work closely together, than if they seldom see one another.

Can you think of two other factors that affect cohesiveness?

_____

_____

_____

Some other factors affecting cohesiveness are the following.

■ **The size of the team**

The larger the team, the greater the number of possible interactions, and the less frequently will any particular member, including the leader, have the opportunity to communicate with any other member. Taking two extremes, a team of two working together may be able to talk together all the time; if you are in a group of a thousand, you may not even be able to recognize some people in the group.

Opinions vary about the best number for a team. However, most people would probably agree that a team with more than 15 members will find it difficult to operate as a single unit and will tend to fragment.

■ **How similar the work is**

If the work is similar the methods and technology are likely to be similar. People doing similar work can discuss their problems and learn from each other. Having the same kind of problems increases mutual understanding and sympathy.

■ **The background of the team members**

If they are similar in age and upbringing, they will find it easier to talk and understand each other's way of thinking. People of different race, or who have a different set of values, may find it harder to get along, unless there is a willingness to understand each other.

It doesn't always happen that way, of course. Many leaders have found that a mixed group of people can form very strong bonds; perhaps you have had that experience yourself. Also, a group that is made up of people very similar in outlook may lack spontaneity and new ideas.

■ **How easy it is for team members to communicate**

Some teams have to overcome communication problems. Multinational teams, for example, may find it harder to work together if the members have different mother-tongues. A dispersed team, where the members work separately, may only be able to talk on the telephone, and then just on a one-to-one basis. The effective use of information communications technology (e.g. video-conferencing and email) can help to overcome this. This situation is seen more frequently nowadays, because of the trend towards 'telecommuting' or 'home networking'.

You may have special problems of communication in your own team: perhaps people have to work at different sides of a ship or at opposite ends of a pipe or tunnel.

Difficult communication tends to increase feelings of isolation and separation.

You may have listed as a separate item 'how well the members get on together'. There may be no apparent problems that can be put down to size, communications, similarity of work or background, and yet the members simply don't naturally get along together well. We've already looked at the question of matching personalities.

Activity 23 · 5 mins

What do you suggest could be done, in each of the following cases, to try to increase cohesiveness in spite of the difficulty described?

Team members doing quite different kinds of work.

_____

_____

_____

A large group, which is working over a wide geographical area.

_____

_____

_____

A team whose members don't have much in common.

_____

_____

_____

If the team members are doing quite different kinds of work it would be a good idea to make sure that each person knew how his or her own efforts contributed to the group's overall task. Also, it could be worth the group spending time discussing, and trying to understand, the individuals' work problems.

Where the group is large, and spread over a wide geographical area, it might be sensible to split it up into smaller sub-groups, each with a team leader, reporting to the group leader. Occasional team gatherings may help to improve cohesiveness. Constructing a shared 'virtual' environment on the World Wide Web might also be appropriate.

The members of a team who don't have much in common could be encouraged to concentrate on the common task. The team leader might find it useful to hold regular meetings where the importance of the team's common task was emphasized, and decisions shared. Once a fair amount of success comes, they may discover they have a lot in common.

So far in this section it has been implied that cohesiveness is entirely a good thing. Are there any negative aspects to cohesiveness?

Activity 24

3 mins

Can you think of any disadvantages arising from a high level of work team cohesiveness? Try to list **two** possible negative effects.

_____

_____

_____

A highly cohesive work team may:

- make it difficult for new members to become accepted;
- be inward looking and resistant to changes to 'our way of doing things';
- be seen as exclusive and awkward to deal with by external groups;
- even become so obsessed with unity that it allows the team's task to be neglected.

Alison Hardingham and Jenny Royal, in their book *Pulling Together* (1994), tell an interesting tale of one team that got on too well together. The team leader even turned down promotion as it meant leaving the team. Two members became emotionally involved, resulting in a broken marriage, and team meetings were described by an outsider as 'like being on another planet'. Eventually, management were forced to break up the team, even though it had been extremely successful.

Generally speaking, a team leader will want to encourage cohesiveness, because strong group bonds increase the likelihood of success. The danger is that success will lead to smugness, reaction against further development and intolerance of outsiders. To avoid these pitfalls the leader must seek to:

■ encourage unity while not discouraging contacts with and ideas from, outside the group;

■ pose new challenges and not let the team rest on its laurels;

■ give every help to newcomers and urge other members to accept them.

5 Developing your team

It might truthfully be said that **a team that is not developing is stagnating**. A work team is composed of human beings and is therefore living and dynamic. No team can afford to be complacent, no matter how successful it is. There is always another match, another day, another challenge.

Activity 25 · 15 mins

Work through the following checklist and apply it to your own team. Think about each point and, if you feel your team is not developing in this particular way, ask yourself whether it could be and should be, and what you should be doing about it.

(You may find that you can't complete this Activity in 15 minutes. You might care to look at it again from time to time. This is a good idea in any case, because the team is continually changing.)

To what extent is your team doing the following.

■ Learning new skills?

_____

_____

_____

■ Tackling new tasks?

_____

_____

_____

■ Developing improved ways of communicating, with each other and with other groups?

_____

_____

_____

■ Striving for higher levels of output and quality?

_____

_____

_____

■ Thinking up new ideas?

_____

_____

_____

■ Finding better ways of organizing itself?

_____

_____

_____

■ Achieving higher professional standards?

_____

_____

_____

■ Setting higher standards of safety or security?

_____

_____

_____

■ Becoming more self-sufficient and supportive of its members?

_____

_____

_____

■ Redefining its objectives in the light of changing circumstances?

_____

_____

_____

■ Improving its methods of assessment?

_____

_____

_____

■ Requesting an increased share of organizational responsibility?

_____

_____

_____

■ Demanding greater resources to enable new targets to be reached?

_____

_____

_____

■ In what other way could the team be developing?

_____

_____

_____

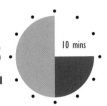

Self-assessment 3

10 mins

1   Fill in the blanks in the following sentences with words chosen from the list below.

The leader has a _____ to:

■ demonstrate a _____ to the team;

■ make clear the _____ of the team members, so that everyone knows what is expected of them;

■ set out the overall and specific aims and _____ , so that _____ knows what has to be done and why it has to be done;

■ _____ objectives wherever possible, to ensure that what is being asked is _____ and _____ ;

■ _____ loudly, criticize _____.

AGREE	COMMITMENT	EVERYONE	FAIR
QUIETLY	OBJECTIVES	REASONABLE	PRAISE
RESPONSIBILITY	ROLES		

2   Select the correct statements from among the following.

a   Conflict is healthy if it is good-natured bantering, or reasoned argument.

b   Conflict can be constructive if it allows people to keep their feelings to themselves.

c   Psychometric testing should be used to make decisions about people.

d   The team leader can quickly learn a team member's personality, with the help of a little concentrated questioning.

e   To get the best from people, you may have to work hard at getting to know them well.

f   One way to assess cohesiveness is to monitor the importance members place on belonging to the group.

g   Difficult communication tends to increase feelings of isolation and separation.

3   Which **two** of the following statements are correct?

Cohesiveness is likely to be greater when:

a   the team is working closely together, rather than separately;

b   there is a greater mix of cultures, rather than when everyone is from the similar background;

c   the team size is above 20, rather than below 15;

d   the work that individuals are doing is similar, rather than when a great variety of jobs are being performed.

You will find answers to these questions on page 121.

6 Summary

- All team leaders must:

  - maintain the trust and support of team members; and
  - aim to minimize interpersonal conflict.

- To tackle the problem of conflict, you will need to:

  - inform team members of the standards of work and behaviour that is expected of them;
  - make sure that team members have an opportunity to discuss problems that arise;
  - take prompt action to deal with serious conflict;
  - keep your manager informed, particularly when serious conflict arises.

- Some useful tips to help the team get on better together are to:

  - emphasize the value and importance of the task;
  - keep everyone busy: a busy team is often a happy team;
  - praise loudly, criticize quietly;
  - encourage friendly rivalry at the expense of hostility;
  - acknowledge the value of the skills and experience of individuals and put them to good use in helping others learn;
  - watch out for the emergence of sub-groups: break them up if necessary by switching assignments.

- To get the best from people, you may have to work hard at getting to know them well.

- Cohesiveness might be measured by the importance members place on belonging to the group: how much effort they would make to retain membership. The factors affecting cohesiveness include:

  - the size of the team;
  - how similar the work is;
  - the background of the team members;
  - how easy it is for team members to communicate: difficult communication tends to increase feelings of isolation and separation.

- A highly cohesive work team may:

  - make it difficult for new members to become accepted;
  - be inward looking and resistant to changes to 'our way of doing things';
  - be seen as exclusive and awkward to deal with by external groups;
  - even become so obsessed with unity that it allows the team's task to be neglected.

- A team that is not developing is stagnating.

Session D
The importance of good relationships

1 Introduction

Every organization is a complex combination of land, buildings, machinery, intellectual property, systems, cultures and, above all, people. The people form a complex organism – rather like a hive of bees – with each person interacting with all the others to a greater or lesser extent, and each making its own contribution to the good of the whole.

This session looks at the ways in which the members of the organization – the bees – interrelate, and the nature of their relationship.

2 A definition of 'relationship'

What precisely do we mean by the word 'relationship'? If you consult a thesaurus, you will come up with related terms such as 'alliance', 'connection' and 'dependence'. So obviously it is some sort of close association between people.

In any organization the nature of that association (or relationship) depends on the structure of the organization and its culture. In small organizations the relationships between people are often relatively straightforward. In large organizations they can be far more complex.

Activity 26 · 3 mins

Imagine that you work in a large organization (which may be the case anyway). Tick all those people in the organization with whom you think you would have a relationship.

Managing director ☐
Directors ☐
Senior managers ☐
Line managers ☐
Section or department heads ☐
Team leaders ☐
Senior employees ☐
Junior employees ☐

You will probably have found that, after some thought, you ticked everyone on the list because, as you will learn later in this workbook, everyone in an organization has the power to influence others, and therefore can be said to have a relationship with them.

3 Formal and informal relationships within organizations

In modern organizations there is a whole variety of relationship structures, ranging from formal, relatively static ones with a defined line of command to fluid ones that are constantly evolving to meet the needs of the business.

We will look briefly at the following four examples of formal relationships within an organization:

- line relationships;
- staff relationships;
- functional relationships;
- matrix relationships.

3.1 Line relationships

In a line relationship each person below the person at the top has one boss and only one boss. Thus a job holder in one position has the power and authority to direct and manage the work of those below who are on the same line.

This establishes a chain of command or line of control from the top of the organization to the bottom. Organization charts are often used to show line relationships and you will probably be familiar with these from work or your other studies. An example of an organization chart for a social services department is shown below.

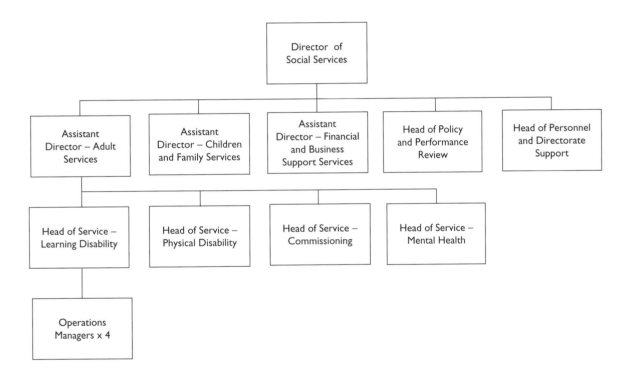

Activity 27 · 2 mins

Do organization charts:

a tell you anything about the people who hold the jobs?   Yes/No

b indicate precisely what the responsibilities of the job
   holders are?   Yes/No

c give any idea of the power held by one person compared
   to another in the same or another department?   Yes/No

You have probably realized that organization charts tell you nothing about the people who hold the jobs or their precise responsibilities. However, they do give some idea of the power people hold as a result of their position in the department and the people they report to. This is known as 'position power'.

So an organization chart tells you the relative degree of power that goes with each job, i.e. how high up the organization the job position is. The higher in the chart, the more power and authority.

The line relationship is found in many organizations, but the move in the last decade or so to flatter organization structures diminishes this form of power. In flat organizations, first line managers carry a very substantial management responsibility.

> The armed forces are a good example of organizations with a strong chain of command. Everyone knows their place. Position power is backed up by strict disciplinary procedures.

Activity 28 · 20 mins

Obtain a copy of the organization chart for your department. Your line manager should have one. Find out how up-to-date it is, who uses it and for what purpose. Does it really reflect the way power is exercised in your organization?

3.2 Staff relationships

Look at this extract from an organization chart of a production department.

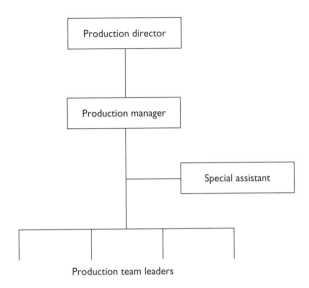

A special assistant, such as the one on the right in the chart, is a 'staff officer' whose job is to act in an advisory capacity in the name of the manager. Part of the role will involve liaising with team members and giving advice during decision making. The relationship between the staff officer and others reporting to the manager is called a staff relationship.

Activity 29 · 2 mins

Use the extract organization chart above to answer the following questions.

a Does the assistant have power over the production team leaders? Yes/No

b Do the team leaders have power over the assistant? Yes/No

No doubt you realized that there is no direct line of control connecting the two. So the answer to both questions is 'No'. Neither has power over the other. The team leaders use the assistant as a source of information and advice but don't take instructions from him or her. They would still be able to go to their manager directly if a problem arose.

3.3 Functional relationships

Functional relationships exist between line managers and functional specialists (those people who carry out specific functions to support the activities of the rest of the organization). Some examples of functional specialists are:

- human resource officers;
- accountants;
- health and safety officers;
- members of the legal department.

In most organizations the human resources department acts in a functional relationship with other departments. It has no power over other departments except when it comes to recruitment, interpretation of employment law and other personnel matters.

3.4 Matrix relationships

It is becoming more common nowadays for employees to work for more than one boss. One possible arrangement is a matrix relationship, shown in the chart opposite.

The project managers in the chart report to the production manager for both administrative purposes and work direction (so it is a line relationship). However, the situation is different for the three team leaders. All three report to the production manager for administration purposes. However, team leaders 1 and 2 both work on the project run by project manager A, to whom they report for work direction, while team leader 3 works on the project run by project manager B and reports to this manager for work direction.

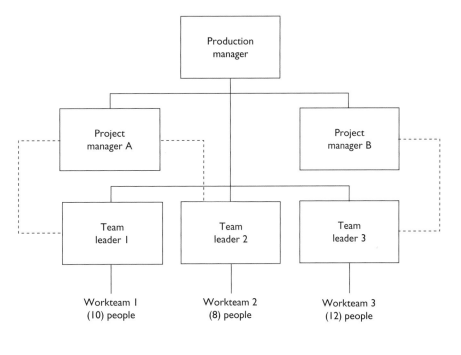

Matrix relationship

Activity 30

3 mins

Answer the following questions relating to the above case.

1   How many managers does each of the team leaders report to?

_____

2   How many people report to the production manager?

_____

You should have seen that the team leaders each report to two managers. Five people report to the production manager.

3.5 Informal relationships

On the organization charts we have looked at, you will probably have noticed that there are no lines running between departments and teams. This is misleading because it suggests that there are no links between them.

From your own experience you know that there is a great deal of communication between all levels within an organization. This is often in the form of informal relationships, but these are never shown on any chart. The reason for this is simply that informal relationships between people in an organization are so numerous that a chart of them would be too complex to be comprehensible.

In larger organizations many of the informal relationships we build internally will be through joining formal or informal groups connected to social activities, or by getting to know people when attending meetings relating to our work role.

Activity 31

5 mins

Make a list of the opportunities that have enabled you to make informal contacts in your organization.

_____

_____

_____

You may have mentioned membership of sports clubs, social clubs, trades unions, and perhaps attendance at such regular events as monthly management meetings, production meetings, safety committee, staff association committee and quality circle meetings.

These informal contacts are invaluable in creating a support network to help you in your work. You can learn more about developing informal networks in the workbook _Influencing Others_ in this series.

4 External relationships

During your everyday job you may sometimes come into contact with people from another department or from outside the organization who have an impact on how you carry out your role.

Activity 32 · 3 mins

Over the last six months what external contacts have you made during your everyday work activities?

_____

_____

_____

_____

You could have mentioned a whole host of contacts, including suppliers, customers, auditors, contractors and specialist consultants.

4.1 Specialist consultants

In the last few years it has become very common for external experts to be brought in on a short-term basis to advise on a particular problem or project. Examples would be management consultants and IT specialists.

It is not always easy to know how to liaise with external experts brought in to work with your team. The lines of authority can be blurred and other members of the team may find it difficult to accept and implement their proposals.

Activity 33

Suppose that your team is involved in setting up a new computer system for one of its existing projects. Your manager calls in a computer expert from an external consultancy firm. How should you interact with this expert? Tick the box(es) that seem correct.

Accept everything the expert has to say and don't ask questions, after all they are being paid to give advice. ❐

Be positive and willing to learn, but don't let your own authority be overridden. ❐

Encourage your team members to ask common sense questions and request clarification where things aren't clear to them. ❐

Test the logic and practicality of what the expert proposes. ❐

Correct any misunderstandings of tasks under discussion. ❐

You could tick every item except the first. When you are dealing with an expert (whether internal or external) everyone benefits if you and your team members feel free to ask common sense questions – it's the best way of preventing misunderstandings arising on either side. And by all means test the logic and practicality of what is being proposed. After all, while the experts know all they need to know about their expert subject, they will probably know very little about your work environment and the way your systems and team function.

You should aim to build a relationship of mutual help and trust between you, your team and the external expert. This will improve your personal power, ensure the commitment of everyone involved, and help to achieve the team's overall work objectives.

5 Differences between people – the effects on relationship building

Towards the end of the Second World War, Dr Eric Berne was responsible for signing the discharge papers of thousands of American sailors. One of his duties was to decide whether each of them was of 'sound mind'. Years later he used his experiences to develop a theory, now known as **transactional analysis** (TA), which is used today by psychoanalysts to shed light on the way people feel and behave.

The theory is that our experiences as children leave an indelible impression on us, and the feelings we have during that period of our lives have a strong influence on our current behaviour. TA is a simple and practical way of understanding and modifying that behaviour.

According to Berne, everyone's mode of behaviour can be classified into one of three groups, or 'ego-states', which he named:

- Parent;
- Adult;
- Child.

Each ego-state has its own characteristics.

5.1 Parent

Parent behaviour is typified by feelings of what is right and wrong. People with dominant Parent ego-states have a strong sense of protection and discipline. They are dogmatic and have controlling personalities.

Parent behaviour is divided into two sub-groups:

- Critical Parent – whose behaviour is typically moralizing, critical, prejudiced and authoritarian.
- Nurturing Parent – who is sympathetic, comforting and protective.

People dealing with them may feel that they are being treated like children; this can be annoying for some, comforting for others.

5.2 Adult

Adult behaviour involves gathering information, evaluating it and using it to make and carry out decisions. It is different from the other two ego-states in that it involves thinking rather than feeling. 'Adults' are typically logical, rational, calculating and unemotional. Others may see them as fair and balanced or as cold, distant and even unsympathetic.

5.3 Child

Child behaviour is spontaneous, controlled by strong feelings of either joy or sorrow.

Child behaviour is divided into three sub-groups.

- Natural Child – who is typically fun-loving, emotional, irresponsible and innocent.
- Adapted Child – a version of Natural Child, which has been toned down to be more acceptable to other people.
- Manipulative Child – whose behaviour is sly, creative and cute.

Such people can be perceived by others as immature, irresponsible, irritating, childish or, at the other extreme, loveable and innocent.

While we are all likely to display all three behaviours at some time or other, the behaviour of every one of us is dominated by one ego-state in particular. However, we can change or adapt any one of them if the circumstances are right.

5.4 How transactional analysis works

Berne represented the communication between people as a 'transaction'. One person sends out a message (or 'stimulus') and the other person responds to it (the 'response').

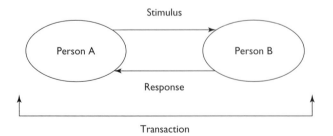

The way in which Person A responds to the stimulus sent from Person B will depend very much on the ego-state of each party.

Transactions can be either 'complementary' or 'crossed'. If they are complementary, then the stimulus sent by Person A will get the expected response from Person B, and both sides will feel on the same wave length.

On the other hand, if a transaction is crossed, then the stimulus from Person A will be met by an unexpected response from Person B, and the message will not get across in the way Person A intends, i.e. the 'wires will be crossed'.

This can be shown in the following diagrams. Each circle represents a person who is behaving predominantly as a Parent, Adult or Child. The arrows represent messages sent between two of them.

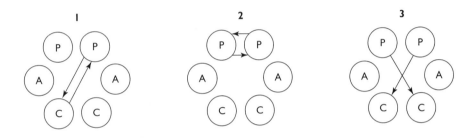

In diagram 1, one of the people acting like a Parent is sending a stimulus to a person acting like a Child. The Parent's dominating behaviour is complementary to the Child's irresponsible behaviour, so the wires are not 'crossed' and the message will be received in the way the Parent intended.

In diagram 2, again the transaction is complementary (Parent to Parent), so the stimulus will be met by the expected response, and the two parties will be on the same wave length.

In diagram 3, the parties have problems. Here both are acting like Parents, and are expecting a response to their message from someone acting like a Child. However, the message they get back is from another Parent, with the result that the wires are crossed. There will be no 'meeting of minds' here. For example, the first person acting as a Parent could be saying: 'That isn't the right way to open the till' while the second person (also acting like a Parent) could respond: 'I know exactly what I am doing, thank you'.

Activity 34

3 mins

Below are three transactions between team members who have dominant ego-states as either Parents, Adults or Children. Draw a line between each transaction and the diagram which represents it. For example, if you think that the middle diagram represents the people taking part in Transaction 1, draw a line between the diagram and the transaction.

Transaction 1	Transaction 2	Transaction 3
Stimulus: 'Do you know what time the meeting starts?' *Response*: 'How should I know? No-one ever tells me anything!'	*Stimulus*: 'Oh, dear! The printer won't work.' *Response*: 'Well I don't know how to do it.'	*Stimulus*: 'Let's see if we can drink eight pints before closing time.' *Response*: Great idea!

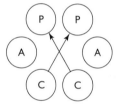 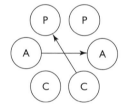 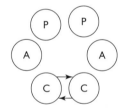

5.5 The value of transactional analysis

An understanding of the principles of TA can help you to manage the relationships between you and your team and between different members of the team.

Thus, while each of us habitually behaves in a particular way (i.e. Parent, Adult or Child), our habitual feelings can be controlled and, if necessary, replaced by more appropriate ones. For example, we can be helped to replace negative feelings of indecision or rebellion (Child), or criticism (Parent) with more positive (Adult) ones.

By understanding the principles of TA, and learning to recognize the habitual behaviours in your team, you can help them to change their unproductive behaviours, to uncross their wires and improve communication and understanding.

Dave has always been a difficult sort of chap. If anything goes wrong with the code he is checking, he will become agitated and say he can't cope with so much pressure. His team leader, Rachel, has never known quite how to handle Dave's outbursts, and they have usually ended up ignoring each other for hours. But, after attending a course on transactional analysis, she decides to try a new approach.

Dave obviously has a Child ego-state. Rachel decides to respond as a Parent to his outburst by saying lightheartedly 'Now hang on, Dave, it's not the end of the world!'. This makes the transaction complementary. She can then try to move him from the Child ego-state to Adult, for example by asking for his opinion or asking how he thinks the pressure on him might be reduced.

By learning how to recognize Dave's habitual behaviour pattern (ego-state) Rachel can respond to it in a complementary way, and then try to change it to a more satisfactory one.

Activity 35

Think about the members of your team. Use the table below to classify them according to their dominant ego-states. Remember, most people have more than one ego-state, but one of them will be dominant.

Team member	Parent	Adult	Child

6 Relationships and organizational culture

6.1 What do we mean by 'organizational culture'?

Organizational culture is the easiest thing to recognize and at the same time the most difficult thing to define.

One popular definition is that it is 'a system of shared meaning held by members of the organization that distinguishes it from other organizations'.

The 'shared meaning' could be about, for example, what it means to be an employee of that organization, or why the organization exists.

The type of relationship between people in an organization strongly reflects the culture of that organization. For example, relationships in one of the armed forces could be very different from, say, a charity. The first is highly structured, with strict codes of conduct, a rigid hierarchy and a highly directive leadership style. The charity would typically be much more collaborative, have a less hierarchical structure and, since it relies to a large extent on voluntary labour, would be very people-oriented.

6.2 Differences in organizational culture, and the effects on relationship building at work

One way in which organizational culture can be classified is according to the organization's orientation. There are at least three types:

- profit-oriented;
- system-oriented;
- people-oriented.

The priorities of the organization are established according to its orientation. For example, in a highly profit-oriented company, profit will be considered to be more important than everything else, and its systems and people will be managed in a way that supports the priority of profit. In contrast, the armed forces are system-oriented, and their systems and people will be managed in ways that support the overall strategy of the organization in either peace or war.

To learn more about organizational culture, you may like to see *Culture and Ethics in Organizations* in this series.

The significance for you is that the organization's culture determines the quality of support you receive from higher management levels in your attempts to build strong team relationships – and the way you go about building those relationships.

A profit-oriented company, which puts little value on its people, is likely to have low morale and a high staff turnover. On the other hand, a people-oriented company (such as Hewlett Packard in the 1980s and 1990s) will put great emphasis on keeping both its staff and customers happy, even if this means that short-term profits may be reduced.

Self-assessment 4

12 mins

I   Draw a line to link each of the descriptions in the right-hand column with its correct name in the left-hand column.

Matrix relationships	Where each person has one manager and there is a chain of command or line of control from the top of the organization to the bottom.
Line relationships	Where a specially appointed staff officer acts in an advisory capacity in the name of the manager and works closely with the team members.
Functional relationships	How specialists, who have authority in certain areas only, relate to the line managers and team leaders.
Staff relationships	Where a manager or team leader reports to two or more senior managers for different purposes.

2   Suggest two ways in which you can develop informal relationships at work.

3   What problems might you encounter in liaising with external experts?

4   What are the three ego-states in transactional analysis?

5   An understanding of the principles of _____ _____ can help you to manage the _____ between you and your team and between different members of the team.

6   Write the behaviours listed below in the correct ego-state boxes.

Parent	Adult	Child

Protective   Spontaneous   Unemotional   Fun-loving
Calculating   Authoritarian   Manipulative   Critical

Answers to these questions can be found on page 122.

7 Summary

- Line relationships exist where there is a defined chain of command from the top of an organization to the bottom.

- Staff relationships hinge on a specially appointed staff officer who acts in an advisory capacity in the name of the manager and works closely with team members.

- Functional relationships describe the arrangement in which functional specialists who have authority in certain areas only, such as accountants and human resource specialists, relate to line managers.

- Matrix relationships exist where a manager or team leader reports to two (or possibly more) bosses for different purposes.

- Informal relationships are a very important means of communication but they aren't recorded on organization charts.

- When dealing with an external expert, you need to develop a culture of trust and co-operation between you, the expert and your team.

- According to transactional analysis (TA) everyone's mode of behaviour can be classified into three groups, or 'ego-states':
  - Parent;
  - Adult;
  - Child.

- You can use the principles of TA to help your team to change their unproductive behaviours, to uncross their wires and improve communication and understanding.

- Organizational culture can be classified into at least three types, depending on the organization's priorities. The types are profit-oriented, system-oriented or people-oriented.

Session E
Building a positive environment

---

1 Introduction

Your position as a first line manager gives you all the formal position power needed to carry out your leadership role. However, there is much more to leading a really successful team than simply having the necessary positional power. To lead a successful team you need 'personal power'.

Personal power is more than just 'charisma'. It is derived from the personal qualities and interpersonal skills you gain when learning to be a good manager.

In this part of the workbook we will look at personal power and the social skills and competencies you need in order to build a strong, united team that has a culture of loyalty and trust.

2 Behaviour breeds behaviour

2.1 The power of behaviour

Your behaviour is important because it may be the only visible indication of your real self – your hidden thoughts, motives and feelings.

> Gordon Spink had been the life and soul of the *Yorkshire Lass Inn* for years. Every night he would buy a round for anyone he didn't know, and then regale them, and anyone else prepared to listen, with his memories of life as a fighter pilot. By the time he died, he had become one of the most celebrated characters in the village, and everyone waited for the fly-past which he had always bragged would be given in his honour when he finally met his maker. Imagine their wonder when it was revealed that he had never been further than a day trip to Calais in a Cessna light aircraft, and that his working years had been spent at the controls of a JCB rather than those of a fighter 'plane.

The only clues as to Gordon's real life and history had been his flamboyant lifestyle and claims of glory. People could only judge him by what they saw and heard.

The way you behave is important because:

■ your behaviour may be the only means that people have of judging you;
■ the way you behave influences how other people behave (behaviour breeds behaviour);
■ you can modify other people's behaviour through changing your own behaviour (remember transactional analysis).

2.2 Your behaviour and leadership skills

As a first line manager you need to develop your own patterns of behaviour so that similar desirable patterns will be inspired in your team. These patterns of behaviour will be the foundation of your personal power.

So how do you do it? What social skills do you need to acquire if you are going to change the behaviour of your team members by your example?

Activity 36

Think of a manager you really admire. It may be someone with whom you work now or have known in the past. Think about how they behave.

What words would you use to describe their personal 'qualities', i.e. their values and beliefs? For example, you might say that they value honesty or that they believe in fair play.

_____

_____

_____

And what characteristics (interpersonal skills) make them so good at interacting with other people? For example, you might say that they show that they are interested in other people, or that they have a great sense of humour.

_____

_____

_____

You may have mentioned some of the following personal qualities and interpersonal skills.

Personal qualities	Interpersonal skills
Loyalty	Ability to inspire
Dependability	Openness
Integrity	Empathy
Fairness	Firmness
Determination	Flexibility
	Humour
	Interest in others

Together these factors make up an overall pattern of behaviour that will contribute to being a good leader.

3 Personal qualities

The way your team behaves depends very much on the way you behave, and you can hardly expect them to be honest, dependable and loyal unless you are the same.

Let's take a look at some of the personal qualities and behaviours needed by a good first line manager.

3.1 Loyalty

Activity 37   12 mins

Martin Sellars leads a team of part-time paid employees and voluntary workers for a large regional charity for the physically disabled. At the monthly management meeting Martin is under fire. The regional director, Frances Dawes, says 'Martin, I have a few concerns about whether your team is delivering the service levels that our clients want. We've had quite a few complaints about your staff not turning up at clients' houses when they've been promised a visit. Is there a problem?'

Martin replies 'My problem is that I've got more volunteers in my team than anyone else. A lot of them aren't properly trained and they often don't turn up for work when I expect them to. It's all very well for Jan, Ravinda and Dave to look so complacent. They've got more paid staff and the pick of the volunteers. If you'd give me a decent team I'd soon show you what I could do.'

Answer the following questions about the above incident.

How do you think Frances will react to Martin's words?

_____

_____

If reports of what Martin has said at the meeting get back to his team, how do you think they will react?

_____

_____

From what you've heard, do you think Martin is likely to do better with a different team?

_____

_____

Martin has shown himself to be a very poor people manager. He doesn't seem to realize that voluntary workers usually need lots of encouragement and support when working in a team with paid employees. The lack of training for volunteers is also a worrying sign of Martin not valuing their contribution to the team.

Frances isn't likely to be impressed and may be thinking that she's made a mistake by appointing Martin to a managerial position in the first place.

If Martin's team hear about his comments, their morale will almost certainly drop. Their performance certainly won't improve and many of the volunteers may decide to leave.

Martin is unlikely to fare better with another team unless he changes his attitude. He doesn't seem to have the personal competencies of teambuilding and relating to and showing sensitivity to others. This small incident could have a major impact on the team. It emphasizes the point that managers who want loyalty from the team must be loyal in return.

3.2 Dependability

Dependability obviously means doing what you have said you will do. This might be in relation to something specific such as 'I will let you have the database entries by Monday lunchtime', or it might be something more wide-ranging to do with the reliability and consistency with which you carry out your job.

Being dependable means that you will put yourself out to meet commitments you have given, and that you are prepared to give someone else's objectives a high priority. But developing a reputation for dependability isn't something you can achieve overnight. Being dependable means that you can be relied upon and will come up with the goods every time. That implies that you demonstrate dependability over and over again.

'Coming up with the goods' cannot just be a question of driving yourself and your team harder and harder to meet other people's deadlines, though this is a situation which you can easily fall into if it is taken for granted that you can be relied upon in any circumstances. Being dependable means being realistic about what you can and cannot achieve and making that position clear. Unrealistic promises about what you can deliver, or regularly giving in to pressure to meet unrealistic demands, will inevitably lead to failure sooner or later, and there goes your reputation for dependability. This is not to say that you should be negative or pessimistic in discussions, but the dependable manager usually brings some cool realism to discussions about what can be done. In fact it is often better to overestimate the time needed to complete a task and then finish it early rather than to underestimate it and finish late.

3.3 Integrity

It is also important for a first line manager to show integrity. This means you should stick to your principles and be honest and consistent. Managers who show integrity get respect.

Activity 38

Manager Dougal blows hot and cold. Most of the time he is lax about discipline, but every now and then he clamps down hard. He urges his team to be honest while being devious himself. He tries to take short cuts to get results and tells his boss one thing while doing another.

The people in Manager Lenny's team always know what to expect. He sets himself high standards and expects his team members to do the same. He tries to be honest and straightforward with the team and in his dealings with his boss. He is firm but fair.

Which manager would you rather work for?

Dougal ❐   Lenny ❐

Most people would probably prefer to work for Lenny. The difference between them is that Lenny is consistent and honest and sticks to his principles, while Dougal isn't and doesn't. Lenny has the personal competencies of commitment to excellence and an ethical perspective.

3.4 Fairness

Activity 39

3 mins

You are a first line manager in a small light engineering company. Two members of your work team want some time off. Jennifer is a good worker, is always on time and rarely asks for time off. Pauline, however, frequently asks for time off and is quite fond of taking the odd day off without permission.

You decide that you could afford one being away but not both.

a Which one should you give the time off to?

Jennifer ☐   Pauline ☐

b On what grounds?

_____

_____

_____

_____

Your inclination may be to give time off to Jennifer, as she rarely takes time off and so is the more deserving case. This seems reasonable and fair.

However, you may argue that you may as well let Pauline have the time off because she'll probably take it anyway. This would be a decision based on expediency, not fairness.

Your responsibility must lie with the team as a whole. When trying to decide actions of this kind, you need to ask yourself: 'If I do this, what will be the effect on the whole team and on the task the team is performing?'

You can't expect everyone to always agree with your decisions, but you need to exercise the personal competence of judgement in these situations. Try to be fair and always explain your reasons to your team members so that you are also **seen** to be fair. This is seldom easy. Perhaps the secret is getting to know your team members really well so that there's mutual trust between you. (You will find tips on how to do this in section 6 of this session.)

3.5 Determination

It is very unlikely that all your decisions at work will turn out to be correct all the time. Like everybody else, first line managers sometimes make mistakes. But you can correct most wrong decisions. Just because you aren't always right doesn't mean that you and your team won't be successful.

Success in team leadership depends upon determination as much as anything else. If you show that you have the persistence to do better and overcome problems then this is one of the best ways to inspire your team.

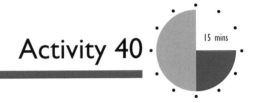

Activity 40

15 mins

S/NVQ
B6

This Activity will help you to review what you have learned so far about personal qualities. It could provide the basis of appropriate evidence for your S/NVQ portfolio. If you are intending to take this course of action, it might be better to write your answers on separate sheets of paper.

a In the following table tick the personal qualities that currently contribute to your management style. Identify any weaknesses and, in the 'Action planned' column, suggest further action to improve these areas. You may like to copy out the table onto a separate sheet of paper.

Analysis of personal qualities

Personal quality	Well developed	Good but could be improved	Inadequate	Action planned
Loyalty				
Dependability				
Integrity				
Fairness				
Determination				

b Think of an occasion in the recent past when you have had to reduce tension between members of your staff and encourage them to focus on the team's main task.

Explain how application of your personal qualities contributed to the success of the situation. Could your handling of it have been improved by an enhancement of these personal qualities? Give specific details.

_____

_____

_____

_____

_____

_____

You could add to this activity by asking someone else in the team to carry out the same analysis of your performance in your role of first line manager.

4 Interpersonal skills

The second aspect of personal power is the ability to inspire openness, empathy, firmness, flexibility, humour and (above all) interest in people.

4.1 Ability to inspire

If you can help your staff to become more involved and personally more responsible for the team's success, their performance will become better and better. You can do this by encouraging them to aspire to the three 'e's: **efficiency, effectiveness** and **excellence**. They must be able to:

- look forward;
- want to be the best;
- know their job;
- take responsibility for their part in moving the team forward.

You can learn more about how to inspire your team in the workbook _Performance Management_ in this series.

4.2 Openness

You have seen earlier in this session that the only clue other people may have to how you are really feeling or thinking is your behaviour. If you are not open about your thoughts and feelings, then people will spend a lot of wasted time and effort trying to guess what you are up to. If you are open and up front about things, then others are likely to respond by being open too.

Gaining a reputation for being open and honest will result in people having much more confidence in your impartiality and fairness. They will then be more likely to look at things in an objective way and be prepared to negotiate constructively when the need arises.

4.3 Empathy

Activity 41

5 mins

Bridget Borland is a nurse at Westland General Hospital and has arrived at work feeling tired and upset. The reason is that she has spent most of last night at the hospital where her husband Liam was taken after a road accident. Having assured herself that his injuries aren't too serious (a broken leg and slight concussion) Bridget has decided to come into work to keep her mind off things.

Miranda is Bridget's ward manager. There have been several urgent new admissions, so she goes over to talk to Bridget as she takes off her coat. The conversation begins as follows.

Miranda: 'Good morning, Bridget. How are you today?'

Bridget: 'Well actually, Liam's been rushed into hospital and I've been up most of the night…'

Miranda: 'Sorry to hear that. Nothing too serious I hope. Listen, we've just had five urgent new admissions and I need you to get started straight away on initial checks for each patient. If you start now, you should be ready to prepare Mrs Jones for theatre by ten o'clock.'

Bridget: 'Well, I'm not sure…'

Miranda: 'I know you won't let me down. Tell me if there are any problems.'

Do you think Miranda did anything wrong? If you think so, how would you have handled things differently?

_____

_____

_____

How do you think Bridget will have reacted to this conversation?

_____

_____

_____

Managers are busy people and it's easy to get so concerned about the job that you forget that team members may have problems of their own.

Miranda showed no empathy – she didn't try to understand how Bridget was feeling. Bridget has had a shocking experience and may need someone to talk to. The lack of understanding by her ward manager is likely to make Bridget feel less inclined to put her best efforts into her work.

Managers who don't empathize with members of their team won't get the best from them. Miranda needs to develop the personal competency of relating to and showing sensitivity towards others.

4.4 Firmness

Firmness is an essential behaviour for every manager. You can only inspire confidence in your team if you are consistent in the decisions you make and constant in adhering to them.

To be firm in this way you need to be assertive, i.e. you need to believe that your needs and opinions are as important as those of other people. Conversely, if you think that your needs are less important, you are showing traits of submissiveness; if you think they are more important, you tend to be aggressive.

Activity 42

5 mins

Look at the following situations and decide what would be the assertive way to deal with them.

1 A new member of your team, Paul, is being confronted aggressively by Catherine, the leader of another team. The confrontation is loud, but Paul seems to be handling it. Do you:

a leave them alone; ❐

b interrupt and tell Catherine that she has no business talking to
    a member of your team like that; ❐

c sit them down and try to reason it out. ❐

2 You and your team have been working together for some time. In general everyone gets on very well, but two of the team tend to argue a lot. Do you:

a insist that they stop bickering and become friends; ❐

b leave it to them to sort it out; ❐

c sit them both down and talk it through. ❐

3 Arthur, a notoriously aggressive member of another department, is picking on Anne, a member of your team who is particularly timid. Anne isn't handling it very well, and you are getting very concerned. Do you:

a order Arthur to leave her alone; ❐

b ask Arthur to come and see you for a chat; ❐

c say nothing. ❐

In all three cases the best approach would be to get everyone involved to sit down and talk about the problem. If you ignore it you would be acting submissively and not giving your team members the support they deserve. On the other hand, if you take an aggressive stance you are simply encouraging the other parties to become even more entrenched in their positions without getting any nearer to a solution.

There are five golden rules for being assertive.

- Decide what you want to say, then say it specifically and directly.
- Stick to your argument, repeating it as often as is necessary.
- Assertively deflect any responses from the other person which might undermine your position.
- Use positive body language.
- Respect the rights of the other person.

Next time you are in a situation where you need to be assertive, follow these five golden rules. It may take some practice, but you will gain an increase in confidence and be able to set a standard of behaviour for others in your team to follow.

4.5 Flexibility

As individuals we often dislike change, but a good manager is always prepared for it.

Firmness and flexibility are two apparent opposites. How can a first line manager be both firm and flexible? Firmness has much to do with knowing what you want. Flexibility is needed in helping you get it.

You need to define your objectives in detail and then be firm about gearing all the actions of the team to meeting them. You need plans to achieve your objectives – but plans often go wrong. This is where the flexibility comes in: you have to be prepared to change your plans as necessary.

4.6 Humour

'If he makes me laugh, I'll probably vote for him. If he makes me think, I won't.'

First time voter at the 2001 general election.

Humour is often greatly underestimated as an interpersonal skill. However, it can be invaluable in creating a bond between you and your team members if it is used in the right way – and if you learn how to use it well.

Activity 43

3 mins

How do you think the use of humour can help you to be more effective as a first line manager?

_____

_____

_____

_____

Humour causes people to listen to you more closely. Humour helps people to learn. It also makes you seem more human, and can be used to make people feel that they are in a 'good' team. Also, people who are cheerful are more motivated and willing to do that bit extra for the team effort.

Some people are naturally funny. Others have to work at it.

Activity 44

3 mins

During the next few days, try out the following ideas.

- Notice how much you smile at people. Then try smiling some more.
- Be more relaxed with your team. Become more concerned, relaxed, open, friendly, interested and caring.
- Notice people whose attempts at humour make you wince. Think about why that is.
- Find out what makes you laugh. Do you have a dry wit or is your humour less subtle? Learn about your own sense of humour.
- Watch people who are naturally funny and have the same kind of humour as you. How do they make people laugh? Try out some of their techniques.
- Keep a note of funny things that happen during the day. This will help develop your sense of humour and provide you with anecdotes to use in future.
- Avoid telling jokes unless you are very good at it. Most people aren't.

4.7 Interest in people

Activity 45

3 mins

How much ought you to know about the individuals in your team? Place a 'Yes' in the appropriate boxes.

What I ought to know about the individuals in my team	As much as I can	As much as I can without prying	Little – it's none of my business
Their ambitions			
Their personal and domestic problems			
Their skills and experience			
Their interests and background			
The problems they may have in terms of equal work opportunities			
Any training they may be undertaking			
Their work problems			

Everything about a person can affect their work performance, so it is wrong to say that these matters are none of your business.

To get your team to respond in a positive way to your leadership, you have to show a genuine interest in them as people and build up a rapport with them.

You should try to know as much as possible about your team's:

> It could be argued that taking an interest in your team members is the most important part of your job as a manager.

- ambitions;
- skills and experience;
- training;
- work problems.

You can take an interest in the other areas so long as you don't pry. After all, everyone has a right to privacy.

5 Emotional intelligence

Emotional intelligence was first discussed in 1990 by researchers in the USA. It involves being aware of one's emotions and how they affect and interact with traditional intelligence (IQ). It has been found that people who are best at getting in touch with their own and other people's emotions are more successful both at work and in their social lives.

For example, research into the sales figures of a group of insurance salesmen showed that those who were 'in tune' with their emotions, who could manage their feelings well and who were optimistic sold 37% more insurance in their first two years than their less sensitive, pessimistic colleagues.

It is believed that emotional intelligence provides the bedrock for all the competencies we have looked at in this session. It is a new and important concept that will play an increasingly significant part in management theory in the years to come.

6 Developing a culture of trust

People will only work at their best when they feel safe.

If there is an atmosphere of trust and mutual respect in your team, everyone will be much more prepared to offer new ideas and try out new skills, knowing that, whatever happens, any response from the rest of the team will be positive and constructive.

But trust is an elusive thing. A great deal of effort is needed to establish it in the first place, and it can be destroyed in an instant.

You know enough about the skills of leadership by now to identify those factors that build trust in your team and those that can destroy it.

Activity 46

4 mins

Look at the words below, and write them in the appropriate boxes.

Factors that build trust

Factors that destroy trust

Rapport	Sarcasm	Respect	Eye contact	Uncertainty
Acceptance	One-way communication	Listening	Shared humour	Belonging
Criticism	Confidentiality	Innuendo	Consistency	Crossed wires
Constructive feedback	Accusation	Openness	Fault finding	Understanding

7 Confidentiality

Dictionary definitions of the word 'confidentiality' usually contain such words as 'classified', 'restricted', 'personal' and 'intimate'. These terms imply something that is secret or personal to the individual involved. But confidentiality also applies in the wider context to organizations and to the people in them.

As a first line manager you will learn many confidential details both about the work you are involved in and about members of your team.

7.1 Organizational confidentiality

Organizational confidentiality is usually governed by your contract of employment, and breach of corporate secrets will often result in dismissal for gross misconduct. In certain organizations, such as health and social services, it is part of the manager's job to share confidential information. For example, a care worker may have to share information about a client with other care workers and representatives from other agencies such as local authority housing departments. In these situations there will be a formal set of guidelines as to who can have access to the information.

7.2 Team confidentiality

You will sometimes receive personal information about your members of the workforce through counselling them during times of personal crisis and stress.

Whenever you become involved in counselling a member of your workforce, you must treat the information in complete confidence.

Activity 47

Think about a recent situation when you have had to handle personal information relating to a member of your workforce. Answer the following questions about how you handled it.

Why was the information confidential?

_____

_____

How did you obtain the information?

_____

_____

Whom did you share it with?

_____

_____

Did you have the authority to share it?

_____

_____

It is sometimes difficult to decide whether a piece of information you have received is confidential or not. In such situations there is a simple rule: never involve a third party without obtaining the permission of the person who gave you the information, or of the person who is the subject of the information.

7.3 Guidelines for handling confidential information

If in doubt about how to treat 'confidential' information in your possession, use the following checklist as a guide.

- Make sure you know what information is confidential and what is for general publication.
- If you are not certain whether a piece of organizational information is confidential, check with your manager – never assume that it is 'open'.
- If someone gives you information in confidence, never pass it to a third party without checking first with the person who confided in you.
- When you are away from your workplace, avoid discussing members of your workforce with your friends or colleagues.
- To foster a culture of trust and confidentiality within your workforce avoid discussing the personal affairs of individuals with anyone else who works with them.
- Never leave confidential notes or documents where others can see them.
- Make sure that any personal information relating to members of the workforce that is kept on a database is not accessible to non-authorized people.

7.4 Handling confessions

Occasionally members of your team may indicate that they want to confide in you something that could compromise you legally. For example, they might have stolen goods from the stock room or money from the till.

Telling you about it might make them feel better, but it puts you in the position of colluding in the wrongdoing.

Activity 48 · 3 mins

Lee is a credit controller in a large finance company. He has asked his first line manager, Sally, if he can have a quiet word with her. He tells her that he has done something terribly wrong and needs to tell someone about it. He says that she must promise not to tell anyone else about it. If you were Sally, how would you handle the situation?

_____

_____

_____

By confessing to Sally, Lee is trying to make himself feel better by passing responsibility for the problem to Sally. But it would put Sally in an impossible situation, with her loyalty split between Lee and her employer. There is only one thing for her to do. Before he tells her anything, she must tell Lee that she cannot promise to keep his secret confidential. This then puts the ball back in his court, and it is up to him whether to 'come clean' with what he has done, or keep the information to himself.

Very often first line managers have access to information that is personal to members of their team but which is held on a corporate database. The type of information varies but, in certain circumstances, could relate to such matters as pay rates, employment history, disciplinary matters or even mortgage applications.

Activity 49 · 5 mins

Make a list of the types of confidential information you have on file about members of your team. Then make a note of how secure that information is from being accessed by unauthorized people.

_____

_____

_____

_____

Self-assessment 5

12 mins

1 Behaviour breeds _____

2 What **five** roles are normally found in a strong team?

_____

_____

3 First line managers who want _____ from their team must be _____ in return.

4 First line managers who show _____ get respect.

5 A first line manager needs to be _____ in putting the achievement of the team's objectives above everything else.

6 Taking an _____ in members of the workforce is arguably the most important job a first line manager in his/her role as _____ has to do.

7 Which **seven** of the following interpersonal skills are the most important for a first line manager to have?

Flexibility	❑
Ability to inspire	❑
Brusqueness	❑
Skill at winning arguments	❑
Openness	❑
Public speaking	❑
Interest in people	❑
Immovability	❑
Empathy	❑
Good body language	❑
Friendliness	❑
Firmness	❑
Humour	❑

Answers to these questions can be found on pages 122–3.

8 Summary

- There are three kinds of need for human contact.

  - Joining and belonging – the need for group contact.
  - Role and control – the need to have a clear role or control of others.
  - Pairing and sharing – the need for individual contacts on a one-to-one basis.

- As a first line manager, you can improve your leadership skills by developing:

  - personal qualities to loyalty, dependability, integrity, fairness and determination;
  - skills at dealing with people that include ability to inspire, openness, empathy, firmness, flexibility, humour and an interest in people.

- According to research into the concept of emotional intelligence, people who are best at getting in touch with their own and other people's emotions are more successful both at work and in their social lives.

- You should never pass confidential information to a third party without obtaining the permission of the person who gave you the information, or the person who is the subject of the information.

Performance checks

1 Quick quiz

Jot down the answers to the following questions on *Building the Team*.

Question 1   The members of a team have common objectives, and are dependent on one another in some way. Name the other three characteristics of groups that are important in making them into teams.

_____

_____

Question 2   Write down two points of reassurance you would make to a manager who said he would be extremely wary of allowing teams to be self-managed.

_____

_____

Question 3   What do you understand by the term 'organizational culture'?

_____

_____

Question 4   If someone were to ask you the question 'Do teams need leadership?', how would you answer?

_____

_____

Question 5   'Forming' is the first stage of development for a team. What are the other three?

_____

_____

Question 6   List three questions that team members may be asking themselves at the forming stage, as a result of the worries and concerns they have.

_____

_____

Question 7   Describe what's taking place at the storming stage of team development.

_____

_____

Question 8   What is the best way to disband a team? Write down two points you would make.

_____

_____

Question 9   What do we mean by 'role stress'?

_____

_____

Question 10   Explain what a group norm is.

_____

_____

Question 11   Give three reasons why a team might fail.

_____

_____

Question 12   What advice would you give to a team leader who wanted the team to get along better? List three points.

_____

_____

Question 13   If someone asked you what were the main responsibilities of a work team leader, how would you answer? List three points.

_____

_____

Question 14   Define 'cohesiveness', and say how it might be measured.

_____

_____

Question 15   How can too much cohesiveness in a team be counter-productive?

_____

_____

Question 16   By learning to recognize the habitual _____ among your team, you can help them to change their unproductive behaviours, to uncross their wires and improve communication and _____.

Question 17   Which type of organizational relationship is involved where a manager or team leader reports to two or more senior managers for different purposes?

Question 18   What are the **three** ways in which an organization's culture may be oriented?

_____

_____

Question 19   Identify **four** of the important personal qualities needed by a good first line manager.

_____

_____

_____

_____

Question 20   How would you define the word integrity?

_____

Question 21   What is the task of the person who plays the role of Mediator in a team?

_____

Question 22   A team will only be really effective if you, as the leader, are able to:

- allocate the team members to the roles that best suit their _____ and _____
- develop an atmosphere of _____, respect and mutual support within the group.

Question 23   How would you define 'empathy'?

_____

Question 24   Suggest two benefits to a manager of using humour.

_____

_____

Answers to these questions can be found on pages 124–6.

60 mins

▫● 2 Workbook assessment

The clerks, typists and secretaries of CastBright Ltd. were a 'team' in that they all reported to the administration manager, Rakesh Ram. But all was not well. A great deal of squabbling went on: there were three distinct 'cliques' on the clerical side, and many memos travelled back and forth over trivial matters. There was a lot of muttering and complaining. It was possible to get the impression at times that people would do anything rather than co-operate with one another.

Rakesh was an ambitious individual, but he was not concerned about the bickering. When asked about it, he would say: 'Oh, a certain amount of conflict and "politicking" is inevitable in a large office like ours. It's nothing to worry about. They get the job done – most of them.' Rakesh tended to shut himself in his office and concentrate on the special projects that he was assigned from time to time by higher management. No formal team meetings were ever held, as Rakesh 'couldn't see the point'. He did admit to himself that he was often disappointed with the response he got from his staff – they didn't all give him the support he would have liked. But he gradually learned to trust three of his team, who effectively became his 'aides'.

The secretaries each reported to more than one manager, and several of the managers were aware that the administration function was less efficient than it might be. Things came to a head one day when an important piece of information was not passed on from one manager to another, resulting in the loss of a big contract. The two secretaries concerned had a very public stand-up argument, each accusing the other of incompetence. Rakesh heard the noise, and he rushed out in a rage and told them to shut up. 'If you ask me, you're both pretty useless,' he said. One secretary walked out in tears, and the other threw a letter of resignation on Rakesh's desk half an hour later. Rakesh later agreed with his manager that he had acted in haste. He regretted his action, which was caused, he said, by stress owing to pressure of work.

Imagine you've been called in as a consultant to CastBright, and given a brief to investigate the functioning of the administration team. You are asked to make any recommendations that you see fit, which would make them into a better team and operate more efficiently.

- How would you set about your task?
- From what you have read, what do you think is wrong with the administration team?
- What recommendations do you think you might make to CastBright management? Explain the reasoning behind your answer.

Your complete answer to this assessment need not be longer than a single page.

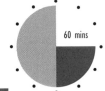

3 Work-based assignment

S/NVQ B6

The time guide for this assignment gives you an approximate idea of how long it is likely to take you to write up your findings. You will find you need to spend some additional time gathering information, talking to colleagues, and thinking about the assignment.

Your written response to this assignment could form the basis of useful evidence for your S/NVQ portfolio.

What you have to do

1 For this assignment, you are asked to provide a description and an analysis of a team you lead or belong to, in terms of the:

a task(s) that it is designed to accomplish;

b type of team that it is: e.g. how many people, how widely dispersed, what skills or disciplines are represented, how permanent it is;

c kind of leadership it has, and how the leader was appointed;

d stages of development that it has been through (forming, storming, norming, performing) and how you, looking back on events, could recognize these stages;

e names of the members, the job-related skills they each provide, and the team roles they fulfil.

2 Then, once you have given some thought to these points, and written down your descriptions:

a say how successful you think the team is, giving examples of what it has achieved;

b explain at least one action that could be taken to improve the team's performance.

What you should write

Write your answer in the form of a report. The whole report does not have to be more than two or three pages long.

Reflect and review

▪ | Reflect and review

Now that you have completed your work on *Building the Team,* let us review our workbook objectives.

■ When you have completed this workbook you will be better able to assess the needs, responsibilities and motivations of your work team.

We have seen that, although all work teams meet certain basic criteria – common objectives and a willingness to work together, with mutually dependent members who are picked and trained to carry out defined tasks – there are many kinds of work team. They vary by their size, location, type of work, type of organization, and so on.

An interesting concept that is currently being put into effect by a number of organizations is the self-managed work team. This is a revolutionary idea, because it challenges the traditional view that managers should control and direct operations, while employees do what they're told.

Most team members gain benefits from work team membership, including companionship, a sense of purpose, and a sense of belonging. This gives us some insight into their motivations: what drives them. As we have discussed, teams are composed of unique individuals, and team leaders must recognize and respect them as such. Successful leaders take time and trouble to get to know their team. Another crucial factor affecting motivation is the organizational culture: the way people are managed and treated, and what is expected of them.

Work teams also have needs and responsibilities. Perhaps their most important needs are clear objectives, committed support from management, and adequate resources. It is the responsibility of every member to communicate; to share in the work; to co-operate with the rest of the team; and to contribute whatever they are able. The responsibilities of the team are to the task, the group and the individual.

Use the following questions to help you decide how best to put this knowledge to practical use.

■ What are the needs of your own team, and how well are they satisfied?

_____

_____

_____

■ Consider the team member who you think is making the least contribution to the team. How could you motivate that person to be more committed to the task and the group?

_____

_____

_____

■ How could you get to know your team better?

_____

_____

_____

Our second objective was as follows.

■ When you have completed this workbook you will be better able to deal with the problems that arise from the way in which people in work teams relate to each other.

The way in which people in work teams behave and interrelate is crucial to the team's success. A collection of individuals, no matter how well qualified they are, will not necessarily make a winning team. We have discussed the question of job-related roles, relevant to the specialist knowledge that people have, and team roles, which are more dependent on their personalities. Belbin suggests that nine team roles can be identified. Whether or not you are able to pick your team, it is worth considering how each of these roles will be filled in your team.

Consider how you might answer the following questions.

■ What problems have arisen that can be put down to the way in which team members relate to one another?

_____

_____

_____

■ How well are team roles covered in your team?

_____

_____

_____

The third objective was as follows.

■ When you have completed this workbook you will be better able to recognize and influence the stages of team development.

You have to know what's happening to influence events. The stages of development we discussed – forming, storming, norming, performing, and (eventually) mourning – take place in every team.

A critical stage is storming, in which people are vying for position and working out their relationships. We noted that conflict can occur, which may be healthy, productive, and constructive, or just the opposite. The team leader must take action should the conflict get out of hand.

It is not easy to predict how long each stage will last, and it's important to watch out in case the team gets stuck in one phase of development.

Try answering the following questions.

■ Thinking back, can you recognize the stages of development of a particular team?

_____

_____

_____

■ Is conflict in your team healthy, productive and constructive? If not, what action are you planning to take?

_____

_____

_____

The fourth objective was:

■ When you have completed this workbook you will be better able to improve the performance of your work team.

One factor that is a key to the success of most teams is the level of cohesiveness. There are many techniques for increasing cohesiveness, such as taking teams away together on events. The team leader has most influence here, and can improve cohesiveness by adopting a positive, enthusiastic and committed attitude.

Performance will be affected by all the other aspects we have discussed, including clarifying objectives, supporting the team, handing over more responsibility, respecting individuals, improving lines of communication, and assessing roles.

Here are some final questions.

■ What techniques, discussed in this workbook, seem to have most relevance to your team?

_____

_____

_____

■ How do you plan to implement these techniques?

_____

_____

_____

_____

_____

_____

_____

_____

The fifth objective was:

■ describe the types of structure which form the basis of relationships in organizations

You should understand the effect of different structures on the way the organization functions, and the way in which some can be static and others change according to the needs of the work. You should also appreciate the importance of developing formal and informal relationships both inside and outside your organization.

You may want to ask yourself the following questions:

- Do I make the best use of the relationships that I have developed?

_____

_____

_____

- Are there any other ways in which I could develop relationships which could make my work more effective?

_____

_____

_____

The final workbook objective was:

- develop qualities and skills that will promote positive team relationships

Behaviour breeds behaviour. By developing certain ways of behaving you can promote harmony in your team and encourage them to adopt working practices which benefit both the workforce and the organization. Things to think about include:

- How far does my own behaviour reflect the interpersonal skills and attributes needed by an effective team leader?

_____

_____

_____

- What practical steps can I take to change my own and my staff's behaviour in order to strengthen team cohesion?

_____

_____

_____

◼ ▣ 2 Action plan

Use this plan to further develop for yourself a course of action you want to take at work. Make a note in the left-hand column of the issues or problems you want to tackle, and then decide what you intend to do, and make a note in column 2.

The resources you need might include time, materials, information or money. You may need to negotiate for some of them, but they could be something easily acquired, like half an hour of somebody's time, or a chapter of a book. Put whatever you need in column 3. No plan means anything without a timescale, so put a realistic target completion date in column 4.

Finally, describe the outcome you want to achieve as a result of this plan, whether it is for your own benefit or advancement, or a more efficient way of doing things at work.

Desired outcomes			
1 Issues	2 Action	3 Resources	4 Target completion
Actual outcomes			

▣ 3 Extensions

Extension 1

Book — *Wisdom of Teams*
Authors — Jon R. Katzenbach and Douglas K. Smith
Edition — 1998
Publisher — McGraw-Hill Education

Katzenbach has become one of the gurus of teamworking, and this book presents stories and case examples involving real people and situations to demonstrate why teams will be the primary building blocks of company performance in the 21st century.

Extension 2

Book — *Gower Handbook of Teamworking*
Author — Roger Stewart (Ed.)
Edition — 1999
Publisher — Gower Publishing Limited

A comprehensive account of the practices and techniques of teamworking.

Extension 3

Book — *Team Roles at Work*
Author — Meredith Belbin
Edition — 1996
Publisher — Butterworth-Heinemann

This book develops Dr Belbin's ideas about his famous team roles. It is not bed-time reading, but is full of interesting and stimulating argument.

Extension 4

Book — *Why Teams Don't Work*
Authors — Harvey Robbins and Michael Finley
Edition — 2000
Publisher — Texere Publishing

Harvey Robbins and Michael Finley explain that teams fail largely because they don't think through the human implications of working in teams. This is a practical handbook that will help team members and team leaders to work together to make decisions, stay in budget, and achieve their team goals.

4 Answers to self-assessment questions

**Self-assessment 1
on pages 17–18**

1 The six characteristics that should be listed in a good definition of a work team are:

b are willing to work together;

e are trained to carry out defined tasks;

g are dependent on one another in some way;

h have common objectives;

i think of themselves as a team;

k go through a selection process.

2 The words were: GROUP, WORK, CULTURE, BASE, LEADER, TEAM, SHARE, TASK.

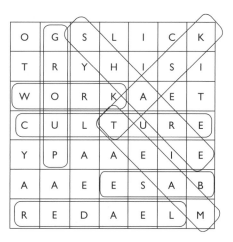

3 a SELF-MANAGED teams need both SUPPORT and training.

b Every TEAM has responsibilities towards the task, the group and the INDIVIDUAL.

c COMPANIONSHIP and a sense of BELONGING are very important motivating factors.

d Self-managed teams must be given the RESPONSIBILITY and authority to achieve their OBJECTIVES, without INTERFERENCE from management.

e PERSONALITY isn't always important: PARTICIPATION is.

Self-assessment 2 on pages 39–40

1 The correct order is: forming, storming, norming, performing, mourning.

2 The correct matches are as follows.

Belbin's team role	Description and contribution to team
5 Co-ordinator	(f) Clarifies the team's objectives and sets the agenda. Mature, confident, but not domineering – a good chairperson. Promotes decision making and delegates well.
7 Completer	(a) A painstaking individual – very conscientious, and often anxious. Will personally check all details for errors and omissions. Delivers on time.
6 Implementer	(h) Is capable of translating ideas into manageable tasks. Well-organized, disciplined, efficient, trustworthy and reliable. Always knows what's going on.
1 Monitor/ evaluator	(d) Another high IQ person (like the plant) who is typically introvert and sober. Good at making sound judgements, and at absorbing and unravelling information.
9 Plant or creator	(b) A creative and imaginative person, who also has a high IQ; original and unorthodox. Solves difficult problems.
4 Resource investigator	(c) A sociable, stable extrovert, who is enthusiastic and communicative, but tends to dominate. Explores opportunities and develops contacts. Needs to be under pressure.
2 Shaper	(g) Dominant extrovert, who thrives on pressure. A good task leader, and has the drive and courage to overcome obstacles. May be charming, and have a lot of nervous energy.
3 Specialist	(i) The expert on the team. Usually an introvert, whose interest is confined to own sphere of knowledge. A single-minded self-starter.
8 Teamworker	(e) As the name suggests, a reliable team player: co-operates willingly, and a good listener and diplomat. Avoids friction and confrontation, and calms the waters. A likeable extrovert.

3 The correct statements are as follows.

a In determining job-related roles, job descriptions are essential.

c A possible reason for failure of a team is that team members are badly selected.

d Roles are important to the individual and to the team. However, the main issue is the fulfilment of the task.

Statement b should read . . . A group norm can be defined as a standard of behaviour that is derived from what the **members of the group** perceive as being acceptable and appropriate.

Self-assessment 3 on page 59

1 The leader has a RESPONSIBILITY to:

- demonstrate a COMMITMENT to the team;

- make clear the ROLES of the team members, so that everyone knows what is expected of them;

- set out the overall and specific aims and OBJECTIVES, so that EVERYONE knows what has to be done and why it has to be done;

- AGREE objectives wherever possible, to ensure that what is being asked is FAIR and REASONABLE;

- PRAISE loudly, criticize QUIETLY.

2 The correct statements are as follows.

a Conflict is healthy if it is good-natured bantering, or reasoned argument.

e To get the best from people, you may have to work hard at getting to know them well.

f One way to assess cohesiveness is to monitor the importance members place on belonging to the group.

g Difficult communication tends to increase feelings of isolation and separation.

3 Cohesiveness is likely to be greater when:

a the team is working closely together, rather than separately

d the work that individuals are doing is similar, rather than when a great variety of jobs are being performed.

Self-assessment 4 on pages 77–8

1 The relationships are as follows.

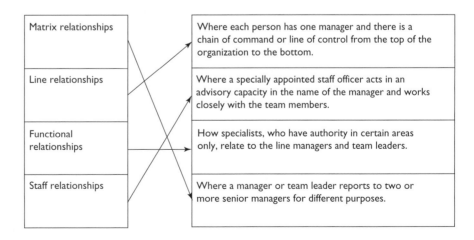

2 Two ways in which you can develop informal relationships at work are through sports and social activities, and through getting to know people at meetings.

3 Problems associated with liaising with external experts include the fact that lines of authority may be blurred and other members of the team may find it difficult to accept and implement their proposals.

4 The three ego-states in transactional analysis are Parent, Adult and Child.

5 An understanding of the principles of **TRANSACTIONAL ANALYSIS** can help you to manage the **RELATIONSHIPS** between you and your team and between different members of the team.

6

Parent	Adult	Child
Protective Authoritarian Critical	Unemotional Calculating	Spontaneous Fun-loving Manipulative

Self-assessment 5 on page 102

1 Behaviour breeds **BEHAVIOUR**.

2 The five roles in a strong team are Achiever, Provocateur, Consolidator, Reflector and Mediator.

3 First line managers who want **LOYALTY** from the team must be **LOYAL** in return.

4 First line managers who show **INTEGRITY** get respect.

5 A first line manager needs to be **FIRM** in putting the achievement of the team's objectives above everything else.

6 Taking an **INTEREST** in members of the workforce is arguably the most important job a first line manager has to do in his/her role as **TEAM LEADER**.

7 The seven interpersonal skills that we looked at in the workbook, and that are generally agreed to be the most important for a first line manager are: ability to inspire, openness, empathy, firmness, flexibility, humour and interest in people.

5 Answers to activities

Activity 4 on page 10

Your rating of your organization may not be entirely fair or accurate, but it does reflect your view as an employee. Would others give the same rating? If the total marks are 30 or less, then you cannot be too enthusiastic about the organizational culture. There may not be a great deal that you can do about it (although you do have some influence!), and you should bear this in mind when you are assessing the morale and performance of your team.

Activity 10 on page 26

The most logical assumptions would be as follows.

	Forming	Storming	Norming/ Performing
A team is seen to be continually arguing.		✓	
The members seem to be excessively polite to one another.	✓		
In this team, the members are discussing, freely and constructively, the value of the procedures they are expected to follow.			✓

6 Answers to the quick quiz

Answer 1   The members of a team are also: willing to work together; go through a selection process; think of themselves as a team.

Answer 2   Among your points may have been two of the following: (a) When people are given power, responsibility, and clear objectives, they tend to take responsible attitudes. (b) Managers do not become redundant by allowing employees to manage their own work; instead, their role changes. (c) Just because teams manage themselves, it does not mean to say that they will be leaderless: most teams appoint a leader. (d) SMTs do not always make the right decisions, but neither do managers; unless and until teams are empowered to make their own decisions, and allowed to make mistakes, they will not grow and develop.

Answer 3   There are many aspects to organizational culture, but essentially it could be said to be the way people are controlled and expected to behave.

Answer 4   You may have answered 'Yes' or 'No' according to your opinion! But a more reasoned answer could be along the lines of: 'Even when teams are set up without a leader, they tend to appoint one, so it seems that teams do need leaders. Reporting, and interfacing with other teams, is also usually easier when there are leaders. And a leader is likely to provide a focal point or "pivot" for a team.'

Answer 5   The other stages are: 'storming', 'norming' and 'performing'. You may also have mentioned 'mourning'.

Answer 6   Among the possible questions are: 'Why am I in this group, and will I fit in?'; 'What are our aims and objectives?'; 'Can these aims and objectives really be achieved?'; 'Am I up to the job?'; 'Am I capable of more than this?'; 'How will my performance be assessed?'; 'How will this group be better than, or different from, the one I've just left?'; 'How will I get on with the leader and with the other team members?'; 'Is joining this team good for my career?'

Answer 7   At the storming stage, the team are trying to establish relationships with one another, and to determine who will take the dominant roles.

Answer 8   You may have mentioned: planning for the end as early as possible; providing a formal opportunity for members to say what they have valued about each other as colleagues, and what they will miss; warning the team that they will feel sad; holding a final dinner or lunch; encouraging team members to stay in touch as individuals.

Answer 9   Role stress can take several forms, including: role conflict, in which two or more roles clash; role overload, which means trying to fill too many roles.

Answer 10   A group norm can be defined as a standard of behaviour that is derived from what the members of the group perceive as being acceptable and appropriate.

Answer 11   A team may fail if: team members are not willing to work together; the members are badly selected; objectives or terms of reference are poorly defined; there is a lack of training or support; communication is poor; there is unresolved personal hostility.

Answer 12   Some points you may have made are to: emphasize the value and importance of the task; keep everyone busy; praise loudly, criticize quietly; encourage friendly rivalry at the expense of hostility; acknowledge the value of the skills and experience of individuals and put them to good use in helping others learn; watch out for the emergence of sub-groups.

Answer 13   You could mention: demonstrating a commitment to the team; making clear the roles of the team members, so that everyone knows what is expected of them; setting out the overall and specific aims and objectives, so that everyone knows what has to be done and why it has to be done; agreeing objectives wherever possible, to ensure that what is being asked is fair and reasonable; supporting the team when things are going against it; supporting the individual (including, if necessary, protecting individuals from the group).

Answer 14   Cohesiveness is a quality that can be used to describe how unified a team is. It can be measured by the importance members place on belonging to the group: how much effort they would make to retain membership.

Answer 15   A highly cohesive work team may: make it difficult for new members to become accepted; be inward looking and resistant to changes to 'our way of doing things'; be seen as exclusive and awkward to deal with by external groups; even become so obsessed with unity that it allows the team's task to be neglected.

Answer 16   By learning to recognize the habitual **BEHAVIOURS** among your staff, you can help them to change their **UNPRODUCTIVE** behaviours, uncross their wires and improve communication and **UNDERSTANDING**.

Answer 17   The organizational relationship where a manager or team leader reports to two or more senior managers for different purposes is a matrix relationship.

Answer 18   An organization's culture may be profit-oriented, systems-oriented or people-oriented.

Answer 19   Personal qualities you could have chosen include:

■ loyalty;
■ integrity;
■ fairness;
■ determination;
■ dependability.

Answer 20   The personal competence of 'relating to and showing sensitivity to others' is important in displaying tact and courtesy to members of staff. You won't get the best from your staff unless you treat them properly and listen to their concerns.

Answer 21   The task of the Mediator is to keep a harmonious atmosphere and resolve conflict within the team.

Answer 22   A team will only be really effective if you, as the leader, are able to:

■ allocate the team members to the roles that best suit their **SKILLS** and **COMPETENCIES**;
■ develop a culture of **TRUST**, respect and mutual support within the group.

Answer 23   Empathy involves relating to and showing sensitivity towards others.

Answer 24   By using humour you:

- encourage people to listen more closely;
- help them to learn;
- make you appear more human;
- make people feel that they belong to a good team;
- motivate them to make an extra effort.

7 Certificate

Completion of this certificate by an authorized person shows that you have worked through all the parts of this workbook and satisfactorily completed the assessments. The certificate provides a record of what you have done that may be used for exemptions or as evidence of prior learning against other nationally certificated qualifications.

superseries

Building the Team

....

has satisfactorily completed this workbook

Name of signatory ....

Position ....

Signature ....

Date ....

Official stamp

Pergamon
Flexible
Learning

Fifth Edition

superseries

FIFTH EDITION

Workbooks in the series:

For prices and availability please telephone our order helpline +44 (0) 1865 474010
or email directorders@elsevier.com